FAR HORIZONS

FAR HORIZONS

A JOURNEY *from* WAR *to* PEACE

AARON TAIT

Hardie Grant
BOOKS

Published in 2025 by Hardie Grant Books an imprint of Hardie Grant Publishing

Hardie Grant Books (Melbourne)
Level 11, 36 Wellington Street
Collingwood VIC 3066, Australia
www.hardiegrant.com

Hardie Grant acknowledges the Traditional Owners of the Country on which we work, the Wurundjeri People of the Kulin Nation and the Gadigal People of the Eora Nation, and recognises their continuing connection to the land, waters and culture. We pay our respects to their Elders past and present.

A catalogue record for this book is available from the National Library of Australia.

Far Horizons: A Journey from War to Peace
ISBN 9781761452796

Publishing commissioned by Courtney Nicholls
Publication managed by Shahirah Hambali
Edited by Alexis Washam and Michael McConnell

Cover design by Amy Daoud
Typeset in Adobe Caslon Pro 12pt by Elysia Clapin
Printed in Australia by Opus Group Pty Ltd, an Accredited ISO AS/NZS 14001 Environmental Management System printer.

The paper this book is printed on is certified against the Forest Stewardship Council® Standards. Griffin Press – a member of the Opus Group – holds chain of custody certification SCS-COC-001185. FSC® promotes environmentally responsible, socially beneficial and economically viable management of the world's forests.

This story is drawn from real events as I lived them, recorded them in my journals and remember them now, years after they took place. I've changed some names to protect privacy and, where necessary, merged or slightly altered some events for security reasons.

Memory is an imperfect witness. Sometimes unreliable, sometimes contradictory and always filtered through the lens of a fallible narrator. What follows is the truest account I can offer, built from old notes, fading recollections and the meaning I've since made from both.

PART I

WAR

- ONE -

Midnight.

The bottom of the Pacific Ocean. My knees sunk into the murky silt of its floor.

Absolute darkness. I held my hand in front of my mask but couldn't see a thing.

"Your fingers are your eyes now," Chief Timms barked at us on the first night of the diving course when a fellow recruit asked for a torch. Then he'd issued the punishment: his slow, torturous version of one hundred push-ups, his tattooed biceps rippling as he glared at us with contempt, moving through his with ease. The first push-up took ten minutes.

And the recruit was now long gone, a marked man from that first hint of weakness. We'd all learned not to ask questions because questions equalled punishments, and we didn't need any more of those.

I was bone tired. Bitterly cold. My fingers were always the first part of my body to go numb. They barely felt like they were part of me during these long, cold weeks. I kneaded them together in a futile attempt at warmth; the thick calluses on my palms (from the countless push-ups and chin-ups) scraped roughly against each other.

An icy stab of ocean crept in through the thin, rubber neck seal of my black wetsuit, chilling my spine. My mind drifted, and I tried my latest distraction technique of tricking myself into believing that I wasn't ten metres underwater in the dark of night: that, instead, I was curled up in a warm bed in the family home I'd left the year before. But that night it didn't work. The water was too cold. I shivered uncontrollably, and my teeth made a rubbery squeak on the scuba mouthpiece that would bring me a short injection of air and an unwelcome chaser of salt water with each breath. My heavy diving cylinder dug into my ribs; after adjusting it, I reached into my wetsuit sleeve, pulled out a dull yellow glowstick and, using the tiny cloud of light it emitted, checked my air gauge. I had another forty minutes left on this dive, a search with our hands along the piers of an old timber wharf to clear it of explosives. Forty freezing minutes. The only good news was that tonight the bombs weren't real, just training devices. So rather than being blown up, the only threat was that if we couldn't find them all on this sweep, we'd be punished by being kept in the water for another few hours and made to repeat the test.

It was the final night of my navy diving course.

I'd been selected from the seventy officers on basic training as a possible candidate for Special Forces, and this was the first step. One of my best mates, Luke, or "Apples", so nicknamed because he came from the apple-growing state of Tasmania, had also been shortlisted, but he'd been deployed up close to Indonesia to help stem the illegal immigrants arriving by boat. The course started three weeks ago, with sixteen candidates, including my other mate, Kel, a six-foot lifeguard, surfer and all-round waterman who grew up on the East Coast beaches. My nickname was "Spud", a play on my surname, Tait, which sounds like the second syllable in *potato*. The three of us had bonded quickly in basic training and had been inseparable ever since. We were the fittest in our class, fiercely competitive and always determined to be the best: to show we had the right stuff. And the best way to do that was to become clearance divers, who then went operational in a real war. Most nights, on officers' course, we would sneak out of our rooms after lights out and creep down to the ocean through the bush like special operatives, for hours of push-ups, running, swimming and breath holds where we would run along the ocean floor in the pitch black with heavy boulders cradled in our arms to hold us down. Apples was resentful that he'd been deployed north and that Kel and I would be taking the first diver selection step before him. But we all knew, like only young men can, that we'd be friends for life.

The three-week course was simple. Learn how to scuba dive, prove you were tough enough to go to the next stage and don't get injured. Of the original sixteen, eight were now gone. A mix of blown eardrums, strained backs, destroyed knees and, for some guys, it was all just too hard. Too cold. Too painful. Some had been bullied off course as the instructors successfully manipulated us to do their dirty work for them and we turned, like a mob, on the weakest. When one recruit had lagged on a run, they made us carry him five humiliating miles back to base. He quit within the hour. At the end of the day, it hadn't mattered what excuse any of the quitters had. The word next to their name was the same: *FAIL*. According to Chief Timms, no matter how hurt you were or how hard things got, it was always your choice. You could grit your teeth, put up with everything they threw at you and take another step towards becoming a qualified Special Forces operative. Or you could fail.

So, we were down to eight men.

Well, seven men and one boy.

I was only seventeen.

A sharp tug on the rope around my waist shook me back to my senses, secured with the bowline knot that we could tie, by then, with one hand behind our backs, underwater and in the dark. We spoke through the rope, using a series of tugs and pulls to communicate, and it was our only connection to anyone beyond our cold, lonely part of the ocean. This message was a signal to stop, that a diver had found a mine and that we'd be here for a few minutes while we waited for orders from the surface. I peered into the black, looking for the dark smudge of another diver, but nothing was clear, so I wrapped my arms around my chest for warmth, closed my eyes and waited for a message. I thought about the friends I'd said goodbye to at high-school graduation the year before. None of them had joined the military with me, so their mothers had likely cooked them dinner tonight. They probably all enjoyed long, hot showers. In fact, very little about their day would have been anywhere near as challenging as what I'd willingly volunteered for, signing up to fight for my country. Lucky bastards. I knew it was probably best not to think about their lives, their easy university schedules and cruisy part-time jobs. My reality was that this was the seventh long dive of the day. I'd been in the ocean for ten hours already. My eyes stung with the salt water that had been leaking into the faulty mask that I had drawn the short straw on at five o'clock that morning. My knee was stiff and dull with the ache of a strain I picked up on the second week but kept running through; an injury that would remain with me for the rest of my life. My head was pounding with the agony of a wisdom tooth that had earlier decided to burst its way sideways through my gum.

But it was my ears that were the worst. They'd never really been great, beaten up by years of surfing and scuba diving as a teenager, but this was a new level of bad. When I descended underwater, my eardrums ached with a sharp stab I'd been grimacing through ever since black blood and mucus started leaking out of my nose a week earlier. I'd had to make a habit of apologising to the guys when I surfaced slower than them, and Kel had been surfacing alongside me so it didn't look as bad, and I wouldn't get failed. If Chief Timms found out how bad my ears were, he would have told me that I was "fucking weak" and sent me to the on-duty nurse. I'd be off diving course in a heartbeat. She would recommend that I get warm. Wrap a blanket around me, make me a cup of tea and recommend some bedrest. Every instinct screamed that this was a great idea.

However, there was a major downside. If I quit now, I'd be a laughing-stock. Both among the seventy classmates I'd just spent basic training with, convincing how tough I was, and worse, among the qualified divers who would laugh at me for a very short moment and then simply forget me. Since the British Navy of the 1800s, those holding the rank of midshipman have been labelled "snotties", as they were said to be so sickly and scared at sea that they wiped their tears and snotty noses on their coat sleeves. Not me, though. I was determined to not be seen as a snotty. And I was not going to fail. I might have been the lightest recruit by twenty pounds, but I could run and swim faster than most of them. I would pass this course and hurdle over this first step on my way to being one of the toughest fighting men in the world. A Clearance Diver in the Royal Australian Navy. A member of a formidable fighting unit that can hold its own with the US Navy SEALs and the British SAS.

Things had started well. Four weeks earlier, on my first day at dive school, I had finished third out of thirty men in a two-mile swim, where we lay on our backs and kicked through the water with long fins on our feet. The sinewy, grey-haired lieutenant commander of the diving school had given me a wink of approval as I climbed out of the water, barking, "You might just have what it takes, Mid", and slapping me hard on the back, rattling my boyish frame to the core. I'd thrust my chest out proudly when I walked away from him. He was right, and I'd been doing all I could since to keep showing them all that I did have the right stuff. But after a few punishments designed to "weed out the snotties", I'd also learned that the best way to survive was to be a grey man and not draw too much attention to myself. Finish every run in the middle of the pack. Complete each dive well, but do not excel; otherwise, there was a long way to fall if you started screwing up. So far, I'd withstood the sleep deprivation, the endless runs and the swims back and forth across the bay. I'd been told that I was a fucking disgrace, that I was pathetic and that there was no chance I'd pass. I'd been pissed on by the instructors, held underwater until I almost drowned and pushed off a boat going so fast it felt like I was hitting concrete when I met the water. It wasn't just me being targeted. The instructors had been democratic and everyone had received roughly the same horrific treatment. But I was still here.

For those last few hours of the diving course, I needed some divine help. Despite growing up in the Pentecostal Christian church, I hadn't prayed for a while, and my adolescent faith had been quickly pushed aside by the harsh realities of life in the navy. But I mustered up the small semblances that were left of my spirituality and brought my hands together to make a shivering double fist. In my mind I uttered a short prayer, asking for help to get through this last dive.

God acted quickly.

Boom!

A loud, muffled thump broke through the night ocean, like a baseball bat hitting a pillow, and a flash of too-bright white light pierced through the abyss. Then darkness re-enveloped all. I peered again into the black, small flashes of lightning sparking across my eyes from the gone-too-soon light. Nothing. The only sound was of bubbles, keeping me alive for a breath before ascending with each exhale, thirty feet above to the real world. I took my regulator out of my mouth and listened. Silence. But then there was a strong tug on the rope around my waist – someone was passing a message through the line. Another tug. Then three more. Five in total. Five tugs meant "emergency", and we needed to surface immediately. That matched up with the bright white light and loud bang, meaning it wasn't God, in fact, but a diver recall device, an underwater flare that meant something was wrong. They'd told us what emergencies this might signal: a shark, an enemy inbound or a dead diver.

I kicked hard to the surface and furrowed my brow to push through the sharp needles that stabbed into my sinuses as I returned to the real world – Sydney Harbour on a frigid and still September night. The navy base looked like most military installations do: dark, mysterious and ominous, but in the hills around it, the city's mansions twinkled like jewels, modern castles that working-class kids like me could only dream of living in. My ears filled with water as usual, my whole head pulsing to recover from the agony I'd just pushed it through again.

Through my blocked ear canals, I made out the muffled yells of Chief Timms for us to "get out of the fucking water now!". The water splashed effervescently as eight divers churned towards the ladder, Kel just ahead of me. With our fins in our teeth, we hauled our tired bodies and our heavy diving gear upwards; then we ran along the old timber wharf that had speared splinters into our hands during many rounds of push-up punishments. We ran past the cold shower we rinsed under each night, which felt warm to our chilled bodies. Past the timber beams, where we had quickly figured out how to execute twenty perfect overhand chin-ups so we could eat. Past the tables where they would serve our food and where they'd once encouraged us to eat triple rations, as "you may not be eating again for a while", before putting us on the most intense run of the course, most of us throwing up everything we'd just tried to get down. Past "the Lizard", a twenty-foot beam of slippery wood extending out over the water that we'd been forced to hang off by our fingertips for hours. "Fuck you, Mr Lizard," I said under my breath, and Kel laughed. I didn't know what we were running towards, but my guess was soft sand sprints in wetsuits or swimming laps of the harbour until sunrise. Or maybe Chief Timms had one final torturous tactic in mind to get a few more of us to quit on the last night.

But I was wrong. We ran into the sick bay. Inside was the on-duty nurse, rugged up in a thick navy-issue blue jacket, a steaming cup of coffee in her hands. She didn't even look up at us; her eyes were fixed on the television. We crowded into the old room – built when the world was last at war in 1942 and barely changed since then – water from our wetsuits dripping into puddles on the chipped concrete floor.

The banner at the bottom of the screen was brutal in its simplicity: *America Under Attack*.

A tall building had smoke pouring out of its upper floors.

Then "Whoooafuckwhatthehellholyshit!" came out of us, a chorus of disbelief as we watched a plane fly into a second tower. Someone backed into me by accident, like the blast had hit them, too. We stood silently, still shivering from the cold, and watched the TV, struggling to grasp what we were seeing.

The first to speak was Chief Timms. "Shit, men," he said, rubbing his scarred, shaved head with his big bear-paw of a hand. "We're all about to go to war."

And he was right. We would come armed, we would come angry and we would come to bring Iraq to its knees.

- TWO -

Six Years Earlier

I HADN'T BEEN able to wipe the grin off my eleven-year-old, whiskerless face since we'd left camp at dawn. I knew that back home my brothers, Michael (two years older than me) and Daniel (five years younger), would be playing armies with the other boys in the street. Pretending to shoot at each other with fake plastic guns, making machine-gun noises with their mouths and dying valiantly as they stormed each other's bases. But on this day, I was on my first hunt with Dad, and the bullets loaded in my weapon were real.

We were spending the next five days out in the rugged and remote King Country of New Zealand's west coast, where snow-capped mountains loomed ominously over dark valleys torn apart by roaring rivers. At breakfast, Dad had spotted a ridgeline where he thought the hunting looked good, and we'd spent five tough hours getting up there. We were after wild pigs and goats, feral animals that had been introduced to New Zealand and were fair game for hunters. I stepped quietly through the undergrowth, my heel striking first and rolling silently to my toes, my socks still wet from a cold river crossing a few hours earlier. Dad was just ahead of me, walking slowly, his thick muscular legs below his All Blacks rugby shorts straining with each light step. He wore his long green woollen Swanndri smock, which was heavy, coarse, and made my skin itch when I touched it. This smock had seen some things, and on rainy days my brothers and I would look through the black-and-white photos of him wearing it on hunts, in the graduation photos of him from a survival course in the navy, and at the end of weeks out in the bush with the Outward Bound wilderness program. This smock had been his only shelter during long dark nights in the wild, kept him warm in the snow and been soaked with blood from animals that he'd shot. It was a man's piece of clothing. My dad's. Our bloodline was from the rugged and revolutionary highlands of Scotland, and our name meant "cheerful warrior". Tait men were tough and could get through anything with a smile and sometimes even a line of poetry to lift the mood.

In past hunts, when we'd been too young to join, Mum would let us stay up late on Sunday night for Dad's return. We'd be in our pyjamas, hair still wet from our evening bath, waiting to hear our car's tires crunching up the stone driveway, a ten-year-old green Mitsubishi Mirage that he'd found cheap in the newspaper. He would walk in wearing that smock, blood and mud up his shins, and a 180-pound boar over his shoulders, its mouth snarling under its tusks, its eyes dead and distant. We'd poke at it, touch its deadly tusks and be amazed that Dad had been brave enough to kill it. Then while we slept, he would butcher it up, providing a freezer full of meat and a welcome relief to Mum as she struggled to juggle the weekly food budget.

During the week, Dad worked as a sales manager for Pepsi. It was a job that wore him into the ground as he drove across town, persuading people to buy more soda so he could hit his sales targets and, in turn, meet the mortgage payments and feed three hungry boys. The only thing more voracious than our appetites was our desire for books, and Mum would drive us to the library each week where we would all fill a cardboard box with as many as we could borrow. There were always stories of adventure with *Asterix*, *Tintin*, *The Faraway Tree* and then *Secret Seven* and *Famous Five*. By age eleven, I'd moved on to stories of explorers and war heroes and dreamed of one day living my own life of adventure. We played out these stories in the backyards and streets of the suburbs where we lived, with the blood, bruises and broken bones to prove it. This love for books was fostered equally by Mum, a schoolteacher, and Dad, whose lifelong dream was to become an author, something he wrote in the introduction to the end-of-the-semester assignment for the community writing course he attended. I was in awe as we read his poems, short stories and essays about the world. But this publication run of one was placed in a drawer as life got in the way and his responsibility to provide for the family took him away from his passion to be in print.

His father once had the same dream for life as well. Known to everyone as PK, short for Peter Kinrod, he too had dreamed of being a journalist and had written long journal entries every day of his youth that we had read every page of. But his father, Jack, my great-grandfather, a navy man who was part of the Normandy landings in World War II, took him out of school and signed him up for the British Navy as a boy sailor, so he was shipped off to the Korean War. After he left the service, still without a high-school education, Granddad PK talked his way into a cadetship at the national newspaper, a job he lost within a week when his grammar skills were found wanting. Devastated, he never wrote another journal entry. Instead, he married my Nana, and then, like his son would one day do, got to work paying a mortgage and feeding three hungry children. I never met Granddad PK; he died at forty of a heart attack without ever becoming the writer he dreamed of being.

Our family had also always been on the move. Dad had attended ten schools in his childhood, and my mother, from a family of

Austrian migrants, was equally restless. So it was for my brothers and me, too; we'd been the new kids often as we'd moved towns in search of new opportunities and in pursuit of a better life. "Carpe diem!" was a favourite saying in my household, my father putting a video recording of *Dead Poets Society* on many a rainy day. We'd been led to believe that Tait boys – well, everyone, really – could work their way out of a tough position and that, with some resolve, you could make anything of yourself. God helped those who help themselves.

While Dad sold his soul and soda from dawn on Monday to dusk on Friday, it was on the weekend that he truly came alive. Our weekends were defined by one of two things: God and adventure, in that order. So there was almost always church. My parents were leaders in the local Baptist ministry, and each Sunday service there was singing, raising of hands, speaking in tongues, faith healings and baptisms. Dad had lasted only a year in the navy; he left when he fell in love with Mum, and in the late 70s they up and left New Zealand, travelling the world as backpackers.

They became Christians at a commune just outside of Athens. They always explained this group to us like it was their hippy time, and their eyes would glisten as they grew nostalgic for this spiritual, nomadic, free-loving group of God-fearing radicals. Throughout childhood, my brothers and I heard them retell their myths from Greece, of polio-twisted legs being miraculously straightened, thousands of fish jumping onto the beach when the community had run out of food and demons being cast out of troubled souls. Ever since the mystical beginnings of their faith, they'd been filled with the "Holy Spirit" and saw it as one of their life's missions to bring others to Christ. They took a more radical approach to this effort than simply attending a few hours on Sunday mornings, deciding to launch their own theatre troop. They named it Acts 1:8 after the Bible verse, which read: "*You will receive power when the Holy Spirit comes on you; and you will be my witnesses in Jerusalem, and in all Judea and Samaria, and to the ends of the earth."*

It turned out for our family that the "ends of the earth" were the town squares, beaches and shopping malls of New Zealand. Life as a radical Pentecostal family of performers meant that, on Saturdays, our two-bedroom house was filled with a dozen Christians getting fully into costume.

As clowns.

They dressed us as clowns, too, and when everyone had their faces painted, their wigs on and their bright clown suits buttoned up, we would all pile into a van, drive to a new location while we prayed together, and then set up a portable sound system and perform *A Clown's Mistake*, a seven-minute drama with a clear message: Christ was the answer, and hell was not a place anyone wanted to end up. The idea for the clowns was a simple one: clowns attracted the kids, the kids dragged their parents over and, hopefully, some of them stepped towards Jesus. One weekend, a performance was delayed by hours as rain poured down in sheets. My parents suggested that all the clowns pray for the rain to break, and in a Moses-like miracle, the skies parted only in a radius of one hundred (perfectly dry) feet. While the rain fell outside the circle, crowds rushed into the dry circle, the biggest ever for an Acts 1:8 performance. Many people became Christians that day, and my brothers and I were all fully bought in as baptised, God-fearing, non-swearing, non-masturbating boys of faith.

But things began to slip for us as we became teenagers, and we began to swap out the worship music for Soundgarden, Pearl Jam, Nirvana and Rage Against the Machine. The anger of these singers seemed a far cry from the dull, non-political suburbs we lived in. I began to explore life away from being "a good boy" and found myself suspended from school for five days when I snuck away from school camp to go surfing. My parents were called into school when teachers had run out of ways to keep me in order. When we strayed from being good boys, Dad would discipline us with a varnished piece of hardwood, its name written in capital letters down the side – "THE ROD". But as a family, we still held hands and said grace before every dinner. Mum and Dad prayed over us as they tucked us in at night and donated 10 per cent of our family's limited budget to support missionaries in Africa.

Sometimes, Mum and Dad would take a break from the Lord as well, and it was time for adventure. Dad managed to find a twenty-three foot–long sailing boat for a few thousand dollars that we refitted and spent weeks out at sea on, sailing out to far islands in the Hauraki Gulf, where my brothers and I would pretend we were Special Forces soldiers and sneak up on the beaches to conduct reconnaissance missions. These play missions set us up nicely for the time when we were finally old enough to go on Dad's hunting trips. He was occasionally employed by the government to cull feral animals that had been introduced into New Zealand by English settlers and had bred out of control, slowly destroying the native ecosystems. My older brother, Michael, started before I did, but on my eleventh birthday, it was decided that I was ready. I had spent many nights in the backyard shooting cans with an air rifle, and when I passed Dad's safety and target tests, I was ready for this day, my first hunt.

I heard a twig snap under my boot and looked down at my skinny legs. They were muddy and bloody, already ripped to pieces by the fields of gorse thorns we'd pushed our way through since morning. I looked up at Dad, expecting him to be angry at the noise I'd just made, but he had his finger to his mouth to quiet me, and then he signalled with his palm for me to come alongside him. I bit my lip to hide the grin that wanted to escape, not believing that he was using these military signals with me like we were at war and he'd just spotted the enemy.

He pointed to his eyes and then down into the valley. I peered a few hundred yards ahead and, at first sight, couldn't see anything of interest, but then scanned closer up the hill towards us and saw what must have been fifty goats a hundred feet away. There were broad-chested billy goats with menacing horns and long, wispy beards, as well as leaner female does and their kids. Dad pointed at me again and pointed to the ground to signal that I would stay in this position and open fire from there. He then pointed to a position a hundred yards away and to the right, below where the herd of goats were resting, with no hint of what was about to hit them. I fought my teeth down over my grin again, thrilled that I understood his plan; when I started shooting from my high location, they would bolt downhill, where Dad would ambush. He signalled pulling the trigger, then showed me two fingers – I was to open fire in two minutes – and then he nodded at me, slapped me on my bony shoulder, chafed raw by my rifle strap, then stood up and ran quietly down the hill to his ambush position. It was straight out of every war movie I'd ever watched.

I started counting down in my head.

119 ... 118 ... 117 ...

I looked down at my weapon, a .22 calibre rifle. I had sixteen bullets loaded and two full magazines in my backpack, but I needed to be economical with my shooting. Bullets were expensive, and Dad was paid per kill, cutting the tails off and bringing them into the environmental office as proof. I knew to aim for the shoulders of each animal, ideally shooting them through the heart for a quick kill. The big billies would be my first targets, as without their leadership, the herd would be confused and therefore ripe for the picking. I quietly brought back the lever action on my weapon, pulling the bolt up, back, forward and down, spying a round as it moved smoothly into the action. Ready.

101 ... 100 ... 99. I lay down in the undergrowth, pine needles sticking into my body, and slowed my breathing.

59 ... 58 ... 57. I wriggled my left elbow into the dirt to find a steady spot and wrapped my left hand one finger at a time around the wooden fore stock of the rifle.

42 ... 41 ... 40. This gun that I had never taken a life with still felt like a toy, no different from the fake ones I played with in the street or the air rifle we used to shoot pea-sized holes into cans. But I knew what I was doing.

36 ... 35 ... 34. I pushed my cheek against the stock and swept the barrel from left to right across the mob of goats. One big billy was side on to me, his muscular shoulder wide and I lined him up in the sights that ran across the top of my weapon.

19 ... 18 ... 17. I slowed my breathing like Dad had taught me and, without looking, pushed the safety below the trigger from the left to the right.

9 ... 8 ... 7. I exhaled one last breath only halfway, held it, and then my index finger curled around the trigger, cold and slightly slick with gun oil.

3 ... 2 ... 1. This weapon was not a toy anymore, and I was no longer a child.

My rifle cracked with the first shot, and a moment later, the bullet thudded sickeningly into the shoulder of the goat. But rather than dropping like a sniper's target would in the movies, the billy convulsed into the air, its legs splaying unnaturally, and then it ran away, belching out a sound horrifyingly like human vomiting. I squinted away the smoke from the shot, the smell of cordite swirling into my nostrils. Then, from down the valley, came the roar of Dad's semiautomatic and far more powerful AK47, and immediately animals started dropping. I popped up to my knee, pulled the lever action of the rifle and aimed at a smaller female. With just a crack from my rifle her neck exploded in a red mist. Reload. A smaller male dropped. Reload, another big male flipped over in the air, dead, its legs up to the sky in rigor mortis. Reload. I hit a younger billy, who rolled down the hill and came to a stop against a tree, its death kicks drumming loudly against the trunk.

Into my sights stepped a tiny kid goat walking around aimlessly and bleating with terror, looking for its already dead mother. I moved away from it, and then my father ran down the hill, a wild man, standing up and shooting from his shoulder. Not wanting to be left alone in this horror, I stood up, spun my rifle to my back, and ran down after him. I ran past ten, maybe twenty, animals dying and screaming, my heart in my throat, and a lump of hot vomit at the top of my chest. I kneeled again and raised my rifle to my shoulder once more, shooting a white female only ten feet away from me who fell clumsily to the dirt. Dad's ambush plan had worked, and the rest of the herd were pinned up against a cliff, and we were elevated above them, only ten yards away. A massacre about to play out. I was heaving in breaths, my thin shoulders jerking up and down and I lurched back onto my ass heavily, gasping for breath, my head dizzy with the shock of what had just happened, the muzzle of my rifle resting in long grass. Right in front of me was the female I'd just felled. A bullet through her neck. Pure white except for the bright red blood pouring down her side. She wailed in fear and pain. Craned her head around desperately to look at me. I still had two magazines in my backpack, but I couldn't bring myself to shoot anymore. Dad picked off the last half dozen. A crack as each bullet left his muzzle, a split-second hiss through the air, and then a thud as it entered flesh. Then the bullets stopped. His second thirty-two-round banana clip magazine was empty, and the only sound in the forest now was this white doe in front who refused to die. I stared at her and Dad made his way towards me and then knelt beside her, holding her head in his bloody hands.

"Finish her off; she's in pain," he said, like he was telling me to take out the garbage.

I shook my head, my mouth palsied to the left, lips quivering.

"Finish her off, son," he said again, more sternly this time. I shook my head thinly again, not breaking eye contact with her. But Dad was getting angry.

"Aaron, you shot this animal; she is suffering; you need to finish this."

The sour vomit at the top of my chest burned up into my throat and still with my muzzle in the dirt, I pulled the bolt of my action up, back towards me, forward again, bolt down.

"No," Dad said shortly. "Don't shoot her; use your knife; it's the quickest way."

No way, I thought, and with a traumatic grunt, I jerked up to my feet and clumsily stepped the five paces to her. Holding my rifle with one hand, I put the muzzle to her head, looked away, and pulled the trigger. *Click.* Nothing. I looked down frantically at my rifle and reloaded. *Click.* Reloaded. *Click.* I was out of bullets. I dropped my rifle to the dirt and wanted to cry, but not wanting Dad to see my tears I fought it back urgently. I felt his hand on my shoulder, then it moved to the knife that was still in its leather sheath on my belt. The knife that had his initials on it, and then mine. And a small inscription: *Far Horizons*. An invitation from him to me: To live a big life. To be brave. To see the far horizon but then set out for it. He flicked it open and put it into my hand. I was shaking my head, my eyes closed.

"Aaron, this is something you have to finish yourself," he said, and he pushed me firmly but tenderly towards this poor animal. I knelt next to her, and looked into her wet, terrified eyes. My shaking hands grabbed her neck, pulsing with her weak heartbeat, and, grunting in terror, I hacked at her throat. There was nothing smooth about what I did, and I sawed my knife back and forth through gristle, veins and arteries. Her scared eyes finally gave way to a forever stare, and I collapsed heavily back into the grass, cradling her bloody neck and head in my arms. I couldn't look away from her eyes, and my frame heaved with tears and snot and fear and horror. I'd been told many times by Dad that hunting these feral animals was a good thing, the right thing. But God, it didn't feel good. I also knew that I would probably follow the family path and join the military to fight more good fights. To be a good man. If it felt like this, I wasn't sure that I wanted more of it.

Dad rubbed his palms in the horrific wound across her neck, then ran both across my cheeks, smearing blood across my face. "Now you're a Tait," he grinned, then gave me a pat on the shoulder and headed off to butcher one of the younger does for our dinner.

It was a brutal initiation, and only six short years later I'd join the Navy myself, like we all did in this family, following my brother. It was this Tait man's turn to head to war, a cheerful warrior.

- THREE -

WARSHIP *SYDNEY* WAS huge: 138 metres of grey steel, advanced fighting systems and deadly weaponry. She had already been to the Middle East for Gulf War One, the scars running down her side testament to a life of rugged service in the oceans of the world. The wharf was an ants' nest of activity, and it had been kicked by Al Qaeda. Sailors raced somewhere to do something; their ballcaps emblazoned with a skull and crossbones on the side and the words "Bad to the Bone". The shrill beeps of reversing forklifts competed with the high-pitched squeal of the main funnel, the engine being prepared for lines to be slipped and for the ship to head out to sea at any moment. She looked intimidating, ready for a fight, but as I looked up at her for the first time, I wasn't sure what was weapon and what was radar. We hadn't learned much about ships in basic training. The sky was dark and angry, but war didn't wait for a sunny day. It was going to be rough out at sea.

I dropped my bags to catch my breath and readjust my uniform. I hadn't worn my officer's whites since starting dive course, and with everyone else wearing their sea-weathered overalls, I felt like the new kid at school in my polished white shoes, tall white socks, white shorts, white shirt and officer hat. My midshipman rank slides, and the empty white space above the chest pocket of my shirt, free from any medals or qualifications pins, showed just how raw I was. I also knew that as soon as I stepped on board this warship, no-one was going to care how tough I was at the diving school. Here I was a snotty, starting at the bottom once again. And this snotty was late. Bad start.

My excuse, if anyone cared, was that it had taken me an hour to get through all the checkpoints on base. On the day following the 9/11 attacks, security was the highest it had been in years, and the Australian military, like many others, was on a war footing. The world had no idea if more planes were going to be flown into buildings, and we all looked to the skies with a newfound suspicion: the passenger airplanes above us were new bad guys in the story. That morning, I'd already moved through three checkpoints, and my body and bags had been scanned, patted down by the military police and sniffed at by highly strung German Shepherd security dogs. I'd received a text message early that morning from the executive officer (XO) on HMAS *Sydney*, the second in command:

Make your way back to ship immediately. We are deploying. Bring your diving gear.

When I'd read it, I'd made a fist with my right hand and pumped it with delight. "Fuck yes!" I'd yelled, waking up Kel, my roommate. He had looked at his phone and had a message, too; he was deploying on HMAS *Kanimbla*. It seemed that young, fit officers with diving qualifications were in high demand. Lucky us. We'd start at the Academy after this deployment, with medals and war stories, and I felt sorry for Apples, who would be sick with jealousy. And already, my mobile phone, the first I'd ever owned, was filled with texts from envious classmates as the rumours had spread about Kel and me and, more widely, about the Australian units that were deploying. Even the South Asian taxi driver who had driven me to the base had asked me that morning if I was "going to fight the terrorists?".

Hell, yes, I was. I'd never been to the United States, and other than a signed baseball glove I'd been given by an American baseball player as a kid, I had no link to the country. But I, like everyone on my diving course, wanted revenge on the "towel heads" who had just attacked New York and Washington, DC. Lucky for us, our government felt the same. We were going to see action. At breakfast, in the officers' wardroom, I'd quickly scanned the *Sydney Morning Herald* while I inhaled bacon and eggs and a flat white coffee:

Troops, including a contingent of elite special forces soldiers, will start leaving within days to take part in the mission to capture Osama bin Laden and exterminate terrorist networks. Prime Minister John Howard warned that Australians could be killed or badly maimed in the conflict.

The initial euphoria from reading that text from the XO had given way to a new nervousness. Not for the war I was setting sail for, but for what the hell I needed to do now I was at the ship. I picked up my two heavy green canvas bags, my hands still covered with cuts and scrapes from the course. Hopefully, I could keep them out of the water for a few days to let them scab up and begin to heal. In one bag were my scuba diving wetsuits, fins, mask and knives. In the other, two pairs of my grey canvas overalls to be worn at sea, steel-capped boots, some pairs of underwear and socks, my running shoes, fitness shorts and t-shirt, one pair of civilian clothes for when we were in port, my Bible, my military and civilian passports, my journal and my hunting knife.

I started up the thin metal gangway that ran from the wharf to the ship, the link between land and sea, and my bags caught awkwardly on the handrail. I stopped to salute the Naval flag, an important protocol never to be missed, and as I did, my heaviest bag slipped from my right shoulder and pulled my saluting hand down awkwardly. I hoped no-one had seen me, but of course, returning my salute was a six-foot-tall, 250-pound leading seaman, his muscles bursting out of his perfectly ironed white shirt, a wide grin creasing out from his thick beard.

"Good morning, sir; you look like you need a hand," he said, grabbing my lightest bag with ease, probably not realising that the other was the heavy one. I considered for a moment to tell him as much, but then decided that would only add a few inches to the hole of embarrassment I already wanted to climb into. The leading seaman was on quarterdeck duty and was the gatekeeper to the ship, determining who got on and where they could go. Beyond him was a buzz of activity. Tall cranes loaded bulging pallets of supplies onto the top decks. Sailors cleaned .50-cal machine guns in the shade of a Seahawk helicopter, the navy's equivalent of the infamous Black Hawk. Constant announcements were made over the loudspeakers. A lot needed to happen to send more than two hundred officers, sailors and their weapons to a war. I stammered out that I needed to see the XO. The leading seaman turned to call him, and I saw him grin and wink at another sailor standing nearby, dressed in grimy, worn-in overalls. *Bad start, Aaron.* The gossip was surely going to spread that this new snotty was as weak and pathetic as all the others.

The rank of midshipman was a bizarre, lonely and confusing position. While technically I was an officer, I was firmly at the bottom of the heap, below even the lowest-ranking sailors in the eyes of most. Despite this, due to navy protocol, all of the sailors on board still had to call officers like me "sir", often much to their disgust. We'd been told in officer training to always maintain the highest levels of "bearing" and to demand respect from the sailors on board, yet we all knew that we weren't getting anything gifted to us. We'd have to earn every drop of respect over the next five years and slowly work our way to at least the rank of lieutenant to be seen as anything close to a leader. At best, midshipmen were ignored. At worst, we were the laughing-stock of the entire ship. So my goal was to bury my nerves and prove myself once again, just like I'd done over and over growing up, when I'd fought to emerge from the shadows and be selected for a rugby team or try to make a crush notice me. I'd show that I was a rare and impressive officer. A warrior. The real deal.

"I'd leave your bags there, sir, and get straight to the XO's cabin," the leading seaman said, shaking his head at me and hanging up the phone. "He was expecting you thirty minutes ago," he added, along with a click from the side of his mouth.

"Thirty minutes ago?" I said, looking at my wrist. There was no watch – I had taken it off going through security. Again, I thought to explain but left it. "Where is his office?"

"We don't call them offices on the mighty warship *Sydney*, sir; we call them cabins. The executive officer's cabin is on the third deck, twenty-fifth bulkhead."

Unfortunately, I had no idea where that was. I decided to pretend I did.

"Great. Thanks for your help, leading seaman," I said, starting off in the direction that felt correct. His big hand slapped down on my shoulder, stopping me in my tracks, the metal button on my rank slides digging into my clavicle.

"Wrong way, sir. You'll want to about-face and head off that way." He turned. "Seaman Maddin, it looks like sir is a bit new to all this," he said to the sailor he'd winked at. "Can you take him up to see the XO? Oh, and sir," he said and smiled at me. "Good luck."

I couldn't tell now if he was taking the piss or if he meant it.

I followed behind Seaman Maddin and shook my head with frustration about the first impressions I was making. The night before, finishing dive course, I'd felt like a hero. We had proved ourselves, even if we were just on the first rung to being Special Forces divers. We were on that ladder now. We were tough bastards. But now I was by myself. I couldn't just blend in with the others. I was the new snotty. Stepping inside the ship, we entered a maze of stairs, cramped corridors and tangles of cables and pipes. I struggled to keep up with Seaman Maddin, who moved with ease, in sync with the others, knowing instinctively how to dodge his way through the stream of bodies. He lifted his feet and slid down the rails of the stairs with both hands while I stepped down as fast as I could, the leather soles of my shoes not as grippy as I'd have liked them to be. I was lost almost immediately and knew that I would struggle to find my way back to the wharf.

But in time, I'd come to learn that a warship was separated by status. Junior sailors lived belowdecks, with up to fifty people crammed into some compartments, sleeping in bunk beds stacked three high. Sailors ate their meals in "the mess". The officers lived in larger, nicer quarters that were on higher decks and were served by stewards as they dined in "the wardroom". The senior sailors lived in between the two, many of them three or four decades into their careers.

I was an officer, but given my status as a midshipman, my home would end up being in the worst compartment on board, right under the helicopter deck, sharing the space with thirty of those also deemed to be the lowest in the pecking order. There was no chance for privacy on a warship, and with engines, weapon systems, radars, sonars, plumbing and supplies for 230 people to survive at sea, not an inch was spared, something squeezed into every space. The smells were strong and of engine oil, cleaning chemicals and fake smoke from the damage control drills that we would practise almost daily for the next few weeks as we trained for war. Soon, the smell of vomit would make its way into the mix as well, right when we hit the first storm. There was never silence; instead, an always-on chorus of the steel hull shuddering as it pounded into waves, bleeps from sonar and radar, announcements across the loudspeakers, and sometimes even the sound of porn flicks being played in the mess.

Life at sea was not for the faint of heart. After a few minutes of following Seaman Maddin, I was knocking on the door of the executive officer. Seaman Maddin ignored my thanks and headed away quickly, his anti-flash bag slung coolly over his shoulder, there to protect his head and hands from burns if the ship was attacked. "Wait!" came a yell from inside. I stood at ease and took a breath. Then I leaned up against the wall, known as a bulkhead at sea, but then quickly decided against it; it was unbecoming of an officer. I checked my shirt was tucked in and reached down to adjust my knee-high socks. I nodded at people as they passed, but no-one nodded back. They were all busy and had places to be. I felt like I had too much saliva in my mouth, so I swallowed, running my tongue up above the top row of my teeth, which I'd forgotten to brush that morning. I'd never liked the first day at a new school, but the first day on a ship was far more intense.

But I steeled myself that this was where I was supposed to be, even if it felt tough. This was the path I was supposed to be on, to leave home and join the military and, ideally, go off to a good war. Fighting Islamic terrorists in the Middle East seemed to fit the bill, a modern-day crusade of sorts. Even President Bush was praying for us.

I'd started officer training thinking I wanted to become a helicopter pilot, but I'd shifted to diving when a Special Forces diver had told me at the bar one night, "You are a fit bastard, and you've got a brain in there. Become one of us." I thought he was a hero and I liked that he said I could use my brain, because he had fifty pounds more muscle than me. While I'd grown up dreaming of being a fighting man, my body, when I joined up, wasn't intimidating anyone. In fact, I had been so scrawny that on enlistment day, I'd snuck out and eaten two double cheeseburgers, just so I would pass the weigh-in. Once I'd signed off on the final tests, I headed to the airport on a bus with the other recruits, my parents crying as I hugged them goodbye. I told them both with a grin that I'd come back a man, and then I tried not to cry myself as I walked onto the bus and sat down on my seat, waving to them only once out the window.

The truth was that I was moving down the pathway to manhood much quicker than I had expected. I'd certainly had to grow up a great deal since leaving home and even more quickly since I'd left officer school for dive course. My school-captain's English was now peppered with swear words. I'd added ten kilos of muscle and bulk to my frame, and my once skinny arms were now tanned and strong, my body taut from eighteen-hour days of intensive physical training. My curly surfer's hair was now shaved close to my head. I'd barely opened my Bible – the navy was not a friendly place for a good little Christian boy. My nightly prayers had been replaced by a browse through one of the swimsuit magazines I could always find lying around in the common areas. A light beer with Dad at home had been replaced with five pints in whatever bar I could sneak into, ten on the weekend. I was trying to decide on the design for my first tattoo. I'd convinced myself that I didn't miss home anymore, and when I did, I'd tell myself that I could tough it out. I'd still get a lump in my throat if I rang my parents, so I'd largely stopped calling. My younger brother Daniel felt a world away from me, and it seemed my older brother Michael, two years ahead of me at the military Academy, was too busy sneaking out to weekend raves to care about what I was up to. Or maybe he was jealous that I was deploying to a war before he was. Becoming a man didn't come easy, and I found if I buried my feelings and kept proving myself, my skin would get thicker and thicker with each day. Now there was a war about to start, and if I played my cards right, I was going to have a goddamn front-row seat. Surely then I'd be a man.

"Come in, Midshipman Tait," I heard from inside the cabin. "You should have been here thirty minutes ago."

I opened the wooden door – a rarity on board, where everything I'd seen so far was made of watertight steel. I peered around the corner to find the executive officer sitting at his polished wooden desk, which was covered in papers. He kept working as I walked in; a fancy golden pen hovered in his left hand over the document on the top of the pile. I cleared my throat and began, "Apologies, sir! We finished the dive course this morning, and I ..."

"I don't want to hear excuses or problems, Midshipman Tait," he said, his head still down. He wanted to get back to his paperwork. "I want you to be on time, every time. Make sure it doesn't happen again."

"Yes sir," I said, and nodded and swallowed heavily.

He didn't look like I expected him to. The title XO sounded so tough, but this guy looked like the CEO of a bank. His gold-rimmed spectacles were pushed down on his nose, and his straight brown hair flopped over his tall forehead. "I'll be quick. *Sydney* is deploying to the Middle East. We are heading north as soon as we can and will do our training work-ups on the way. I need divers and good men for my boarding team, and your name came up a few times when I called around. It sounds like you did well on dive course."

"Thank you, sir," I replied, my shoulders pushing back an inch.

"You are probably too young, but are you leaving anyone behind? Married? Kids?"

Thanks to a youth of Friday nights spent listening to pastors telling us to save ourselves for marriage, I hadn't even kissed a girl. While I'd had plenty of crushes in school, I'd always been too shy to do anything about it. I shook my head.

"Got a will sorted?" the XO asked.

"No, sir." I shook my head again. It wasn't something I'd thought about in my seventeen years on earth. And other than my two bags of clothes that were with me, a guitar, and some sporting trophies back home at Mum and Dad's place, I didn't own much.

"Get one immediately," he said. "There is a legal office on the base. That is your first priority today. We've got a delay on sailing, and you are not getting back on board or deploying with us unless you have a will signed by a lawyer. You have two hours to get that done. Understood?"

Paperwork? That was the most important thing to do before going to war?

But then it got more interesting. He told me that I would be joining Black team. A specially formed fourteen-man noncompliant boarding unit tasked with aggressively boarding Iraqi ships trying to break the already established United Nations embargo. I would start as a reserve in the team, but if he heard good things from the Lieutenant, if there were injuries, or if any of the other guys proved to not be good enough, there was a chance that I would be bumped into the regular group. The team was going to be made up of a blend of qualified Special Forces clearance divers, as well as the best weapons experts and engineers on board. We would use HMAS *Sydney* as our operational base and deploy in helicopters and attack boats every night to take ships. On the way to Middle East, we would be trained in close-quarter combat, specialised weapons, chemical warfare and fast-insertion methods. A feeling of pride overwhelmed the nerves I'd felt when I'd stepped on board. My breathing slowed, and my lips came together as I exhaled long and heavy. A year ago, I'd been popping pimples and studying for my high-school exams; I'd just finished basic training, where I'd spent most of my time marching around a parade ground and ironing my uniforms.

I was standing in the "at ease" position; but rather than holding an outstretched palm in my fingers behind my back, one hand held the other in a fist. The cuts from dive course stung, but I liked the pain. I even felt one open up and begin to bleed again. I couldn't believe I'd been selected to deploy. I'd see action, come home with medals and make the men of my family proud.

"One last thing before you see yourself out, Midshipman Tait," said the XO. "How old are you?"

"Eighteen, sir," I lied. I was still seventeen for a few more weeks, but everyone seemed to be too busy to be checking, and I certainly wasn't going to be bringing up that fact.

"Jesus Christ," he said, shaking his head and looking up, taking off his glasses and blowing his fringe up with a deep breath. "The Captain has a son your age. Look after yourself up there, won't you? It could get a bit dicey. Go."

- FOUR -

Guns wasn't smiling anymore. His stubble was seventy-two hours thick, probably the same amount of time since he'd slept. Our recent transit through the Strait of Hormuz, the strategic pinch point between Oman and Iran – and one of the most aggressively militarised regions on planet Earth – had kept him busy. The black bags under his eyes seemed to droop even more under the tactical red lighting we used at night now we had gone operational, which helped us to maintain our night vision, and also made it harder for the smugglers to spot us. Tall and heavyset, he seemed to subsist on a constant stream of coffee and toast. "Gather in close, men," he said, silencing the hangar. We were a few hours away from entering the official warzone close to Iraq. This was the final briefing before our first mission. He got his nickname because, as a lieutenant commander and warfare officer, he literally controlled the guns on the ship, missiles and cannons that could be used to destroy land-based targets, and enemy planes or ships. But on this mission, these weren't the targets he was after. Instead, it was his job to stalk smugglers using satellites, drones and radar, and then deploy our boarding teams out to take them.

I looked around at the men who made up the two non-compliant teams, named simply Black and Gold. Our dark blue uniforms that were once crisp and new were now worn from heavy use, and our tan steel-capped tactical boots were encrusted with sea salt from the training boardings we'd run on friendly ships as we'd steamed eight thousand miles north. No-one said why, but in the boarding teams everyone shaved their heads and grew their beards out. I'd done the same to fit in. A nostril hair-singeing blend of WD40, jet fuel and diesel was ever present; I could taste it in every meal.

Our mission became clearer us as we had travelled north, and the leaders of the USA, UK, Australia and other nations in the "Coalition of the Willing" had coordinated their response to 9/11. We were brought up to speed with PowerPoint briefings and expected to keep notes. We were operating under United Nations Security Council Resolution 661, passed a decade earlier in the turmoil of Gulf War One. The resolution had been enforced to the letter in the years after Iraq invaded Kuwait, but in more recent years, it had become less stringently enforced, and the UN program had been corrupted. President Bush and Prime Ministers Blair (UK) and Howard (Australia) had obviously seen the resolution as a useful loophole, whereby military forces like ours could strictly enforce a siege on Iraq and soften them up for the ground invasion that was likely coming next. What we knew based on the experiences of the boarding teams that had come before us was that the target was big smuggler ships coming out of Iraq, filled with oil to be sold on the black market. These ships made a run for it at night, and according to international law, we could only board them in Iraqi waters. That meant if we couldn't get inside before the smugglers steered for Iran or Kuwait, we became pirates and faced the real risk of being imprisoned in both a jail and a very tricky diplomatic situation. Our goal, therefore, was to break our way inside the ships as quickly as possible, take control of the steering and change course back into international waters.

And, of course, try to stay alive.

Their job was to do everything they could to stop us, which, over the years of the embargo, they had become very good at. The PowerPoint slides that covered the risks were delivered matter-of-factly, and no-one seemed to make a fuss of them, so neither had I. Death or injury, if it was coming for me, might be in the form of drowning when I climbed up a guardrail that had been deliberately cut through, or I could also drown in a vat of oil with a trapdoor set up for me to fall through. I could burn up if the smugglers were able to throw a bucket of fuel on me and light me up, a particularly nasty way to go. Or be blinded by a fire extinguisher placed above a door and set to go off when I walked through it. The quickest death, though, particularly if Al-Qaeda were involved, was that the boat would be loaded with bombs, and we'd all be blown into pink mist as soon as we boarded. If I were honest with myself, though, as we'd sat in those briefings, I had been more concerned about not making the team, of not proving I had the right stuff, than of being injured or dying in these ways. I'd given away no emotions or tried to make any jokes to make myself feel better. I'd just kept notes in my notebook, and played it cool.

On the way north, we'd learned how to use Broco cutters to slice through the locked steel doors of the smugglers in a waterfall of liquid metal sparks. We could board smugglers either from fast attack boats by slinging grappling hooks up with caving ladders attached, or from a helicopter by fast-roping down a sixty-foot rope without a harness. We'd been skilled in hand-to-hand fighting, as well as close-quarter combat, so we could reach for and use the right weapon in the dark, confused passageways of smuggler ships. We'd learned how to survive chemical warfare attacks and had felt the peppery sting of tear gas in our eyes during training runs. I'd loved every second of the training; it was literally my boyhood dream. But so far, it'd all been just that – training. Now it was real, and we needed to be ready tonight. Well, at least the team did; I was still in the reserves. To be expected, really. I had only just turned eighteen, and even though I'd been working hard to impress everyone, I thought they still saw me as a snotty.

"This operation is now officially live," Guns barked as everyone crowded in quietly. When he spoke, we all listened. The warfare officers and sailors, hidden away in their dark operations room surrounded by radar screens, satellite imagery and drone feeds, had the information for the war, while us boarding teams were the chess pieces that they played across the Persian Gulf.

"Once we cross into the area of operations, nothing is training," Guns growled. "Every boarding is real now, and for you guys, they are likely to be non-compliant. Every second, you need to be on your A-game." He scanned the room and cleared his throat. "Last night, some Yanks went missing up here. We don't know if they have been taken hostage, shot, or if the poor bastards are floating face-down in the drink. *Sydney* will be helping the US Navy look for them, but we'll likely still deploy you guys tonight because, according to intel, there is a mass of ships readying to make a run in the coming days."

I listened carefully, but I was detached, like a reserve player who hadn't made the lineup for the game. Rather than fear, I felt frustration that I wouldn't be going out tonight. I'd tried my hardest to impress everyone, but I was probably still too young.

Guns wrapped up the briefing, told us all to do a final check on our weapons and then get some rest. The first mission was probably in a few hours.

"Spud, stay back," said Lieutenant Hughes as everyone stood to leave. The nickname that Apples and Kel had given me in basic training had stuck and travelled with me on board HMAS *Sydney*. I didn't mind. I preferred to be called by my nickname rather than just "Mid", which implied I was like every other midshipman. I liked Lieutenant Hughes. He was a few years ahead of me, a fresh graduate from the Academy I'd be headed to next year, and a soon-to-be family man – his first baby would be born while he was on this deployment. He was square-jawed with his blond hair shaved short; one of those officers who was as fit, strong and capable as any of the sailors he led.

The other men filed out of the hangar, and I made my way towards the Lieutenant. A few slapped me on the shoulder, and someone threw in a "Good luck, Spud", which got some laughs. From that first day on board, when the XO had told me I was a "reserve" in the team, I'd been determined to lose that label. Since then, I'd given my all to be promoted to the mission-ready unit. I'd tried to be the first to arrive at every briefing and the last to leave the pack down for each training mission. Every fast-rope run from a helicopter had been as quick and as perfectly executed as possible. I asked Keg, one of the experienced navy divers, for extra weapons training so my drills were smooth and fast. It wasn't leaving room for much sleep because while many of the other guys in the team were full-time on the boarding team, I was doing double, meeting my boarding requirements while still doing eight-hour shifts up on the bridge of the ship, completing my navigation training – technically, my actual job on board. I'd been getting two to three hours of sleep a night, which, on top of the dive course, had turned reality into a fuzzy smudge. When I needed to, I could find a reserve of cortisol and focus on the job at hand, but when I got a moment to myself, a dull numbness took over. There was no time to think about what I was doing or where I was going. Making things a little more complex was that, for weeks, I'd quietly pushed through the agony of two ruptured wisdom teeth, knowing that reporting them to the docs would have me scratched from both the team and the deployment.

"Spud, how are you doing?" Lieutenant Hughes asked me, smiling.

"Great, sir."

"No need to call me sir when it's just us," he said, quieting his voice. "You've done well these last few weeks. You've impressed some people."

"Thanks," I said, nodding. I looked straight at him. Was I being pulled from even the reserves, and redirected to back up on the bridge?

"You know how the XO told you you're just a reserve?" he said, meeting my gaze. "Well, that's no longer true. We've pulled someone who wasn't good enough, and you're in. You'll be partnered with Crokes as a cutter. You carry the equipment, and Crokes will do the cutting. We'll be relying on you guys to get us inside any vessel quickly. It's a big job. You'll be in my team. Any questions?"

"No," I replied, shaking my head. I felt a satisfied smile begin to crease across my face, my lips still together. But that satisfaction gave way to something else entirely. A sharp heat trickled through my body, from my spine out to my fingertips.

"There's no need to head to the bridge for duty; I've chatted to the navigator to get you off that for now. Go get some rest in case we go out later. Stay safe." He slapped me on the shoulder and walked out into the reddish darkness, back into the bowels of the ship. I watched him go. Like Guns had said at the start of his brief, the shit was about to get serious. That applied to me now, too. Chemical weapons. Terrorists. Suicide bombs. Drowning in oil, or the ocean. So many ways to die. Was I in over my head here? Was the team going to barge back into the hangar, laughing at the prank they'd just pulled? The dive branch liked screwing with our heads like that. Or maybe someone more senior was going to say, "Wait a minute, this kid just turned eighteen! He's too young for all this!" But no-one came. I was alone. This was real. And it still felt like the right thing to be doing. That this was the right fight to be in. My great-grandfather Jack had died two weeks earlier, but before he'd passed, he written from Scotland about how proud he was that I was "seeing action". I'd never met him, but I'd been bursting with pride when Dad had passed on his message by email.

I made my way out of the hangar and headed for my sleeping rack, my left knee still sore from dive course; probably one more injury I'd keep for life, however long that was going to be. I wove my way through the maze of bunks squeezed tightly together and came to my thin mattress, my only refuge on board. I took my boots off, placed them in my locker, and then pulled myself up with a handhold and slid my way into my tight space. I lay flat, took a deep breath and turned on a tiny Maglite torch so as not to wake anyone. A small circle of light scanned across the photos I had of my high-school buddies, taken the year before. I was a young boy in them. We all were. And while a lot had happened since then, I didn't feel too far from that young boy. I looked at pictures of my parents. What would they think if they knew what I was doing now? I'd been playing it all down to not worry them. I was just one young officer on board a big warship, and I wasn't doing the dangerous stuff. Which so far had been true.

I reached for my Bible, tucked beside my mattress. I hadn't opened it since I'd been on HMAS *Sydney*. The strength and inspiration that religion gave me as a teenager seemed so far from real life now. But with a movement of old habit, I flicked it open, challenging God, if He existed, to give me something useful. I flicked through the pages and stopped randomly. I closed my eyes, circled my index finger in the air and then pointed at a verse.

Be strong and take heart, all you who hope in the Lord.
(Psalms 31:24)

I closed the Bible and stared up at the base of the bed above me, just twelve inches from my nose. They packed us in tight on board. I repeated the line in my mind.

Be strong and take heart.

Be strong and take heart.

I liked the "be strong and take heart" bit. I just didn't know how much hope I had in "the Lord" anymore. I felt more that it was going to be on me to make it through what lay ahead. That I would be strong. Focused. That I would do what I was sent here to do, and I would do it well. That I would be part of the most effective team in the Gulf, and we would stop these smugglers. Help take down the terrorists. I wasn't convinced God played a role in much of that; I'd have to help myself get through what was coming next. Tonight there were dead Americans who, last night, were doing the job I was about to start.

I turned onto my side, my shoulder almost up against the rack above, opened my journal and began writing.

If you are reading this, something bad has happened to me up here, and I won't be coming back. There is a will with the lawyers back in Sydney, but I don't really own all that much, so this letter is probably more important.

I wrote for the next twenty minutes. About being thankful for my childhood, and for all that my parents had done for me. I wrote about the hopes I had for my life. To maybe make a positive difference one day with a similar passion that my parents had dedicated to their community work in the church. My desire to travel the world. To live a long life. To marry an incredible woman. To see those far horizons Dad had always talked about and move towards them.

"Be strong and take heart," I murmured to myself.

I closed my journal and my eyes and tried to get some sleep.

***

"Black and Gold boarding teams. Alert thirty, defence stations!" came the announcement over the intercom. The ship accelerated and turned to port so hard that I almost fell out of my bed. This was it. Breathing drowsily through my nose, I forced my eyes open and sat on the floor to lace up my boots. I saw the hatch open and another boarding team member ran out. I raced out after him, through the narrow passageways and past sailors rushing to their weapons, helo and boat stations. In the hangar, I grabbed my black tactical backpack from its hook. Lieutenant Caslick yelled orders over the roar of the Seahawk helicopter. The ship was still pitching and lurching as it raced towards the smugglers, and we all tried to get ready while keeping balance, our feet wide to brace for each time we pounded into a wave. It was rough out there.

My climbing harness was the first thing on, and I stepped my boots through it, pulled it up to my waist and wrenched the buckles tight around my thighs. If we'd be abseiling through a smashed window, I wanted to make sure I was secure on the rope.

I slipped my ASP baton into its holder. If I used this tonight, it'd explode a smuggler's elbow or kneecap. We'd trained the rules of engagement countless times now. We used our hands if we thought we could take down an attacker that way. An ASP baton if we needed something more brutal. Or our gun if they had a weapon. If we needed to make a decision like that, we'd have seconds, and it would be in the dark. I didn't have time to think about that now though. Half of the team were already dressed. They must have slept in the hangar, something I should have maybe done.

Next was my thigh holster, and I pulled in the straps tight. I gave my 9mm Browning pistol a quick check. It felt smooth and familiar. We'd shot, stripped and cleaned our weapons every day of our trip north. It slid in easily to its holster, the canvas already worn away from our training drills.

I looped two cable-tie handcuffs onto my belt, designed to take smugglers out of operation once we had them on the floor, and then pulled my heavy flak vest out. By the briefing whiteboard the lieutenants were talking about the missing American sailors. I listened intently without looking. They'd been found.

Dead. Lying face down in the Persian Gulf. They weren't shot. They'd drowned. I didn't want to drown. I looked over at Keg in the darkness, a qualified Special Forces soldier and so named because he was built like a keg of beer. He was all business as he smoothly checked his weapons, then pulled the bulletproof plates out of his vest. I guessed that he wanted to move swiftly and also wanted to reduce the risk of drowning if he fell in the water, so I quietly and quickly did the same, breaking the rules given to us by the officers, but happy to do so if Keg was.

I took a deep breath through my nose. *Hurry up, Aaron, don't be the last one to be ready.* I checked that my Oakley ski goggles were taped onto my helmet. Flight gloves on, and then leather work gloves hooked onto my belt in case we fast-roped by helicopter, which would be the difference between us sliding down perfectly or falling to a broken back or legs. Radio earpiece in, comms confirmed. Then a quick check over from Crokes, who I was teamed up with. He was a big guy, half a foot taller than me, seven years older and a true "grey man", someone who kept quiet and got on with the job. His strong arms were not covered in tattoos like the others. He didn't sleep with the prostitutes in port like many did in our first port visit in Dubai, choosing instead to have a few quiet drinks with his mates and, where he could, a call home to his wife and baby. He was capable and safe, and I hoped we'd make a good team. I wondered how he felt being lumped with me, the eighteen-year-old midshipman.

The job of a cutter was to find a weak spot in the ship and then use our Broco machine to slice a way in as quickly as possible so everyone could get inside. Crokes would do the cutting while I looked for weak entry points and reloaded the machine each time the rods died out. He checked over my gear, pulled firmly on the straps of my harness, ensured my weapons were secure, and then gave me a slap on the top of my helmet. I checked him, too, but didn't slap him on the helmet. He was taller and bigger than me.

The call came that we were going by boat, Captain's decision. In his opinion, the boats were safer than helicopters. We moved down the internal passageway single file without speaking and came out onto the port side of the ship to a cold, stormy, moonless night. The bosuns, crusty sailors who spent their days and nights out in the elements, readied to lower the boats, seven metres long with aluminium hulls and rubber sides. Fast and manoeuvrable. Fatigue and adrenaline pulsed through me in equal measure, and I wondered if Kel would be going out tonight as well. He was in a boarding team on HMAS *Kanimbla*, another ship that was up in the Persian Gulf. He was probably the only person from my life before this all happened who could understand my reality right now.

"All right, men!" Lieutenant Hughes yelled over the high-pitched whine of the main engine. He walked down our line, checking our gear again – but not our bulletproof vests – and gave us the details of the mission, exactly what we had trained for. A group of smuggler ships had broken out to make a run through the embargo, and there was a strong possibility they were full of oil. They would do everything they could to stop us, but our job would be to board, take control of the ship and crew, and then a steaming party would take them to a holding area to be processed, where the ship would be sold and the crew charged or sent home. The Lieutenant was a good leader. Intelligent, capable and liked by the men. He gave last-minute directions to key members of the team, like a football coach in the changing rooms before the big game. He reminded us to be careful, but the reminder wasn't necessary. By now, we were well aware of the risks; we expected all of these missions to be fast, dangerous and confusing. I was still pinching myself that I'd been selected to be part of this. I looked down the line at the men. We looked mean in our gear, ready for the first mission for all of us. These smugglers didn't know what was about to hit them.

I pulled my sleeve back to check my watch. 2:12am. My radio earpiece crackled to life, something we were all issued with to communicate with each other as a team, with the Lieutenant passing on updates to the war room of the ship using an extra set of comms.

"Men, we're nearing the end of Ramadan, and the inside word from intel is that there could be some bomb boats out there tonight. These things are exactly what it sounds like. They wait for us all to get on board and then fucking ka-boom! It is a very real threat. If you see anything that looks suspect, let me know immediately through the radio, and if I say abort, your number one priority is to get off that boat as fast as you can."

A sarcastic comment came from down the line. "Thanks for the comforting words, boss." It was one of the tough senior divers, and his joke was met with some low chuckles. Maybe everyone was as nervous as I was.

"Okay, men, time to load up," the Lieutenant said in response.

I took a deep breath and made my way down the twenty-foot wood and rope ladder. I was fifth in line. Foaming black waves tore below me. I glanced up at the ship, which from this angle looked bigger than ever, a slab of steel that dwarfed our rubber attack boat. The ship's helicopter took off and roared away overhead. At the bottom of the dangling ladder, I waited for the boat to rise up with a surge of the ocean and then let go, falling hard and grabbing a curved, wet and slippery metal handhold with a white-knuckle grip. The weight of my backpack pulled me awkwardly back towards the gap between the boat and the ship, a seething river I did not want to find myself in. I moved aft to my seat behind the helmsman and sat down heavily, already drenched by freezing water. The remainder of the team made their way into the boat, some of them smoothly, some not, and then the bowman released the thin line of rope holding us to HMAS *Sydney*.

We came up to speed quickly, the bow lifting up high and our stern digging so low into the water that it felt like my boots were only inches from the angry wake racing away from us at forty miles per hour. Pulling away from the relative calm the ship had created for us, the ocean had an abrupt mood swing. My spine rattled as the boat tried to punch its way through a relentless barrage of waves, forcing us to keep our heads low. I gripped the handrail tightly and pushed my legs against a slippery, wet floor that refused to give me any feeling of security. It was chaos. We were either airborne, hurtling off a crest or slamming down hard on the water, the boat shaking with each impact. Any fear about the mission and the reports of bomb boats was sidelined by the effort to hold on and grind our way through the beating we were taking. I turned my head, trying to catch a breath through the spray pouring into the boat and rubbed my tactical goggles with the back of my gloves, but it was useless. It was like being underwater; I couldn't see a thing, and I couldn't think about anything else other than holding on and trying to keep warm.

For twenty minutes, we battered our way across the Persian Gulf like this. Then our speed dropped off, and we all lurched forward with the change of momentum, a stern wave catching up to us and drenching my boots. There were oil rigs around us, dragons of commerce breathing fire into the night. What I would come to learn this whole fight was about. And a few hundred yards away, a dark mass. A smuggler, all of its lights off in contravention of the laws of the sea and the United Nations embargo. Our helmsman maneuvered the boat into its wake, which left a phosphorescent glow for us to follow. Gold team was just ahead of us. Lieutenant Hughes, standing by the helmsman in my boat, updated the brief through our earpieces.

"Black and Gold, this is Chief. Five possible contacts. Gold goes first. Black, stand off at the ready. Eagle will be above as support and lighting if we call for it. Gold, you have seven minutes from now. Go, go, go."

In seven minutes, the smugglers would be in Kuwaiti waters, and if the Gold team hadn't got in by then, they would need to abort the mission immediately. Gold's boat sped up, and they were quickly by the port side of the huge ship. I knew all of these guys well; now they looked tiny and vulnerable, their grappling hooks snagging onto the guardrails. It was all happening like the movies I watched as a kid – a group of sailors storming a ship under darkness. Strangely, though, it didn't feel real for me yet. Like I wasn't actually a few miles off Iraq, fighting in the War on Terror, the next "Go, go, go!" directed at me. The helicopter hovered over the smuggler, illuminating the deck. Our men clambered up rope ladders and swarmed across the ship like crabs scrambling along a beach looking for a hole in the sand. Sparks began to fly, the cutters began slicing through steel hatches, and I felt a jolt of pride. That was my job. Two others smashed at a window with sledgehammers.

"Fucking hell, sir, there are ships everywhere!" our bowman yelled over the roar of the helicopter, his face ghostly green from the halo of his night-vision goggles. I looked around but couldn't see any of them; they all had their lights off.

"Sir, word in from Command," the radio operator reported to the Lieutenant. "We have ten smugglers inbound, time on target – six minutes."

In training, there had only ever been one ship to board. We knew where it was and what to do, and a "smuggler" was a ship from our navy, its crew Australian sailors wearing Middle Eastern dress and attempting Arabic accents. But ten smugglers, real ones and all at once, was not something we'd trained for.

"Sir, fast boat moving this way at speed from the port side!" the bowman yelled. A fast boat likely wasn't a smuggler. In training, fast boats were terrorists.

"Who the fuck is that?!" the usually composed Lieutenant shouted as he clambered to the front of the boat. "Comms, radio in to command that we need to know what's going on here! How many boats can you see, bowman? Driver, are we in Kuwaiti waters yet? Team Gold, what is happening, over?" His scatter of questions was met with silence. Everyone was confused.

I peered into the night, beginning to make out with my naked eye the boat that the bowman had seen through his night vision. "Sir, it's there!" I yelled to the Lieutenant, pointing. The boat was coming in quickly, but it was too dark to make out who they were.

"Chief, this is Gold! We have access through the starboard bridge door, making entry now!" came a report through our earpieces. The Lieutenant shook his head. It was looking messy. He hesitated for a moment, then pressed the radio button on his shoulder.

"Gold, this is Chief. Abort! Abort! Abort! Get off now! Abort! Abort! Abort!"

I pushed my earpiece deep into my ear, trying to hear their response. Silence.

"Chief, this is Gold, we are inside, over!"

"Listen, you bastards!" yelled the Lieutenant.

I guessed that the ship coming quickly was either a terrorist with a bomb or a Kuwaiti Navy ship that could technically arrest the Gold team as pirates now. "Gold, this is Chief. ABORT! ABORT! ABORT! Get off the ship port side. NOW!"

My eyes were glued to the fast boat, which was now on the starboard side of the smuggler. I could just make out a tall ladder being hoisted and then men climbing up. Our guys had got the message now and they were running across decks to the port side, back to our ladders. There were cracks of small arms fire and muzzle flashes, not from our guys. Shots fired on mission one!

"Sir, new word in from command," said the radio operator. "Order is to abort. The Americans have told us that there's a Kuwaiti warship in our vicinity."

It was the Kuwaitis shooting at the smugglers.

"Too fucking late," yelled the Lieutenant.

Ten seconds later, new orders were relayed through from Command. Our turn. I gritted my teeth. I couldn't believe I was doing this. Our boat kicked like a bull, and we were straight up to full speed, heading into the black night, looking for our smuggler. I gripped tightly to the handle in front of me and readjusted my pistol holder, which dug into my thigh through my drenched pants. Crokes slapped me on the leg and held up two fingers in front of my eyes. We had two minutes before we boarded. I passed the message to Keg, the Special Forces soldier who hadn't talked to me once in the four weeks that I'd been on HMAS *Sydney*.

"Let's get these fuckers. Make sure you get us inside, Spud!" he said. There was a gleam in his eyes. He was loving this. I nodded to him, my mouth open just a crack, and I knew that my eyes were wide and wild, too.

"Go! Go! Go!"

Be strong and take heart.

Then someone pressed fast-forward on the world.

In seconds, we were alongside a large and filthy oil tanker. Everyone was yelling and clambering, and the waves were splashing. Somebody screamed, a sickening crunch of bone and flesh as their hand was crushed between our boat and the smuggler. I was next – I pulled myself up the makeshift ladder. The helicopter pushed a storm of wind and noise down on us but also lit up the deck. Oil drums lay on their side with barbed wire on top of them, designed to slow us down. I managed to hop over the barrels, and Crokes and I were quickly by the port bridge door.

"Starboard side all shut up, looking for entry with climbers," came a voice through my earpiece.

I pulled on the long door handle, but it only gave an inch – they'd tied it shut from the inside. Crokes put his shoulder up against the door and grabbed the handle, too. I counted to three, and we gave it everything we had. We hit a moment of resistance, and then, with a crack, the door jerked upward. We were in.

I radioed the team: "Port side open, making entry." I followed Crokes into the bridge, and in the dark we came face to face with our first smugglers, the bad guys who were going to try to kill or injure us, and who we'd been trained to shoot, hit with our batons or take down with our hands. "Towel heads", we'd been calling them. There were five of them, black blurs in the unlit space, and we were all frozen, trying for a moment to figure out who was going to attack who.

Then big Crokes took control and yelled loudly, and then I did, too. "Get down! Get down!" Three of them ran down the stairs, but two fell to their knees, hands in the air, pleading for mercy, screaming, "Please, USA! Please, USA! Please, no!"

I went straight for the ship's wheel and felt a prickle of distrust. *Was one of the pleading smugglers going to attack me from behind?* I grabbed the wooden helm and brought the ship to port, and the bow moved as I hoped it would. Glancing over my shoulder I saw Crokes keeping guard on the two smugglers. They were still yelling, "Please don't kill us, USA."

Crokes pulled up the Velcro patch on his shoulder to show them the Australian flag. "We are Aussie; you are okay."

I yelled out the official words that I'd been taught in my navigation training: "I have the ship." If only my classmates could see me now. My first command. In the Persian Gulf. A warzone. And it was Crokes and me that got us inside, and we didn't even need to unleash the Broco cutter.

"We have the bridge and the ship," I said into my radio. "Request numbers through port side."

Ten seconds later, our men streamed through the port entry and down the dark corridor. We looked impressive. Dark silhouettes, covered in weapons and equipment, moving quickly and quietly. I couldn't see any faces – just black helmets with goggles up and shotguns raised.

"Do you have control?" Lieutenant Hughes said as he ran in.

"Yes sir, I have steering, and I'm down at four knots now."

"Well done, Spud!" he yelled, as he banged the engine console twice with his fist and then let out a big breath. Minutes later, a report came through our earpieces that all smugglers on board were under armed guard in the ship's mess – twenty of them – and that the ship was full of oil.

I stayed on the helm for another few hours and watched the sun rise across the Persian Gulf, a smoky orb of pink in a dusty haze. I was wide awake, feeling like we'd won our first game of the season and I'd played my part. I'd proved myself as a man, in this team and in this war. I wanted to go out again as soon as we could and do it all again. Experience all those feelings of excitement, bravery and camaraderie we'd just been through together.

When the sun was high and the day hot, we were relieved by a steaming party, a group of sailors from our ship who would take the smugglers to a holding area for processing. The sky was a brilliant blue as we tore across the glassy sea at forty knots. All of the men stood, vanity pulsing out of us. We raced up alongside HMAS *Sydney* and half the crew were out on the decks, waving their hats to cheer us. "Bad to the Bone", our unit anthem, played out across the loudspeaker, and the skull-and-crossbones flag flew with a snarl from the top of the mast. We did a lap of the ship at speed, and it was diesel and salt and cheering, and it was every war movie I grew up watching, but now I was in it. The XO was there to greet us, and as I stepped on board he shook my hand. He told us the score: Black team, 1; Gold team, 1; US Navy SEALs (who were out there with us that night), nil. I shook my head and laughed.

We cleaned our gear and then I was down for some rest. At my rack I untied my boots, stripped off my wet clothes, rolled them up and hung them next to the mattress to dry. I overheard two of the guys talking; one of the guys in the Black team hadn't handled the boarding well and had already been pulled. "Fucking pussy" was the description I caught before I pulled my curtains shut. I had no sympathy, though. Him being out meant I was in, and I'd do everything I could to stay. I didn't want just one boarding, I wanted loads. And I wanted this feeling again. I wanted more smugglers as soon as I could. Tonight, even. I wanted medals on my chest when I started at the Academy. I wanted this fight.

In bed, I closed my eyes to try to get some sleep, but it didn't come easily. Moments from the boarding flashed through my mind. The shots from the Kuwaitis and the smugglers' bodies they probably hit. The terror in the eyes of the smugglers when Crokes and I had entered the bridge. The mangled hand crushed between the boats that luckily wasn't mine. I shook them away, not useful. Boarding one of many more to come. My pulse was still quick, and I felt it boom in my neck. My head felt tight and hot, like I'd had five coffees. I needed sleep, but it wouldn't come. *Be strong and take heart.*

- FIVE -

FOURTEEN OF US were once again squeezed into a 7.6-metre attack boat, bobbing like a cork in the ink-black ocean. Fourteen young men who had found themselves caught up in a foreign war far from home.

The biggest, most dangerous smuggler in the Persian Gulf was out there somewhere that night, and we were waiting to take it. Soon, I'd hear those three words through my radio, and it would all be on again: "Go, go, go." But for now, close to midnight, it was quiet.

The ever-present flames of oil rigs licked the horizon – the reason for all this. The nights had turned to weeks, and the weeks to months, and the danger became routine. We always deployed after sunset. It was always treacherous getting on board the smugglers, trying to scale a twenty-foot wall of rusted steel, moving quickly through the ocean at night. Once we were on board it was dangerous as well, as we kept an eye out for barriers and booby traps and fought our way inside. But we'd got it down to a fine art, and based on the numbers of ships boarded, we were the best team in the coalition forces by a long stretch, catching more smugglers than the British and the Americans combined. The US Navy SEALs had been stood down after going too far on a boarding, apparently killing some smugglers, perhaps retribution for losing some of their own. The fear of the early boardings had subsided after the first five or ten, and by now I felt like I lived in a strange mix of enough numbness to not reflect too much on what I was doing every night, and enough sharpness to be sufficiently alert to survive each mission.

The short days of R&R in Bahrain and Dubai didn't live up to expectations and brought neither rest nor recovery. I was part of the diving team that would clear the wharf for mines before we came alongside. We worked in filth, with sewerage pouring into the water from overhead pipes, and dead animals floating by. When we were alongside I either stayed on board to fulfil my security watch duties as an armed guard on the upper decks – no-one wanted a repeat of the USS *Cole* terror bombing that took out sixty sailors the year before in Yemen – or I was out drinking too much in the bars and brothels that our crew were always able find even in the strictest Islamic cities. I was still too shy and nervous to join my mates and indulge in the Russian prostitutes, unsure how to even put on a condom to protect myself from the sexually transmitted diseases we were briefed on. But drinking expanded that numbness in my head, and took away the sharpness, both welcome. My Christian pastors would have been disappointed in me. My Bible remained unopened since I'd read the "Be strong and take heart" verse, and emails from my parents went unanswered. I figured that they were sending enough prayers up to Jesus on my behalf, and I didn't want them to know what I was actually doing on these night boardings. Their stress and anxiety wouldn't change anything; I just had to get myself through it all.

The mission was going well. We'd shut down much of the network by seizing most of the biggest ships and the smugglers were increasingly resorting to local wooden dhows, which were much smaller. But our boarding teams had had plenty of close calls. Guns in faces. Hands crushed. Legs broken. Near-drownings. Bizarrely, my closest scare had come from a possible biological weapon; a parcel I had opened was filled with a white powder, anthrax being the suspect and a new favourite tactic for terrorists. I'd come down with a chest infection almost immediately, a chemical weapons unit had deployed on board with chemical suits and oxygen tanks, and President Bush was briefed personally on the situation. I was quarantined in the sick bay. A brief moment of respite in the exhausting routine of boardings, scuba dives and watches on the bridge of the ship, but unfortunately too much time to think. Mostly about whether I'd survive this possible anthrax scare, or if I'd soon die some other way – by falling into the water in a boarding and drowning, or at the hands of a smuggler who wasn't going to surrender as easily.

Later that night, I was given a pocketful of medicine and sent out on the next boarding. There was no mention of it ever again, from anyone.

Tonight, as we waited, the only noise was the waves slapping up against the hull of the boat. No-one spoke. We'd used up all our jokes, past missions never got brought up and there was no benefit in talking about home and the people we missed – for me they felt a world away, like they wouldn't understand my reality and I didn't want to worry them.

My earpiece crackled as Lieutenant Hughes pressed his button to speak, and he began to brief us for the next mission.

"Okay, boys, tonight is the one. The target is *Fal 12*. Biggest smuggler in the Gulf. No-one has been able to catch it for a decade, even though everyone's tried. Black and Gold teams are both go. Expect every trick in the book and a few that aren't. Climbers, she's huge, so get as high as you can, get set up quickly, and then look for an entry window. I reckon you might be our best bet. Cutters, Spud and Crokes, you will be key tonight." I sat up taller. "Satellite images show she's locked up tight, so use every rod you've got. If climbers and cutters can't get inside in seven minutes, we abort. Eagle is inbound with extra weapons and will provide cover from above. Let's do it. Two minutes."

Our boat sped up and I could see the dark smudge of *Fal 12* a mile away. I unholstered my pistol, checked it quickly, reholstered. Pulled the straps tight on my backpack. Pinched my tactical life-jacket to check the gas cylinder was still attached. My breathing slowed, deep through my nose, mouth closed. I pulled my goggles down and focused on the smuggler ahead. Then came a horrible thought like a bolt of lightning: *I am going to die tonight.* I bit my lip hard, shook my head. *No. No. Be strong and take heart.* A tap on my shoulder from Crokes, his middle and index finger crossed over. Thirty seconds. I passed the signal to Keg.

"Go, go, go!"

We took the port side, Gold hit them from starboard. *Fal 12* was huge, and the deck was way too high for our regular ladders. Grappling hooks were thrown, catching precariously on metal guardrails, and then we were climbing the skinny metal caving ladders, shotguns first to provide cover, climbers second, then us, the cutters. Crokes went before me, the Broco cylinder on his back, and I followed closely, a line of us pulling ourselves to the deck like spiders up a web. Nearing the top of the ladder, it swayed wildly with a downdraft from the chopper and slammed me angrily against the side of the ship. My hands crunched sickeningly against the steel hull, but there was no time to care about the pain. I looked down a long way to scc our boat being swamped by a huge wave, veering away from the side of the ship, the ladder still hooked to it. My whole existence closed in on the few feet of caving ladder above me. Nothing else mattered. Either it held and I made it, or it snapped and I'd sink like a stone, my lifejacket not good enough to hold up the double load of cutter rods I was carrying tonight. The ladder twisted again like a furious crocodile and my back slammed against the side of the ship. I held on with everything I had.

"Crokes!" I grunted. "Crokes!" My backpack was hooked onto something, and it was pulling me away from the ladder; my fingers were starting to give way, millimetre by terrifying millimetre. The deck was just above me but there was nothing to reach for. It was all just two feet away, too far.

Then a bear-claw of a hand reached down and grabbed me by the top of my backpack. It was Crokes; he was flat on his stomach and pulling with all his strength to heave me up and onto the safety of the deck. Below me, the cursed ladder snapped and fell into the murk. We had only five more minutes. I looked at Crokes, but there was nothing to say; we ran for the bridge as fast as we could with the weight on our backs.

"Man in the water! Repeat, man in the water! We do not have a visual on him." The report was hard to hear above the chopper, my heavy breathing, and our boots clanking on the deck. No name was passed. The helicopter broke its hover to find him, taking away our light and aircover. Crokes and I hurtled our way across the deck, the barbed wire and oil tank barriers harder to navigate in the dark.

"Attempting entry starboard side," came an update from the Gold team.

"Black cutters making our way to port bridge wing," I added. Other than my close call on the ladder and the man in the water, we were okay, and everyone was moving quickly, going through the motions now, like every other boarding we'd done. We could take this thing. We ran up the stairs, two at a time, and at the bridge wing door, I kneeled, threw my backpack onto the floor and pulled out the first Broco rod. Crokes pulled down his welding mask; I lit the tip of the rod, and sparks waterfalled over us as he got to work on the hinges. I glanced past him through a small window with bars across it and caught sight of men running around in the darkness, screaming in Arabic. The bad guys. The smugglers. The pricks who were going to try to stop us. Usually, they didn't put up much of a fight, and these guys were probably no different.

"Climbers ready," came a report from Mike. He was a guy as smooth as silk; he'd smash his way inside in no time. Their ropes unfurled metres away from me and pulled taut as they kicked off and abseiled down. Perfectly timed, they swung back in towards an exposed window at the front of the bridge and struck the glass cleanly with their sledgehammers. The window shattered but didn't break enough for entry. Glass rained down on the deck twenty feet below. Crokes's first rod fizzled out, and I reloaded the tool quickly, sparking his flame and then pulling on the door with everything I had to see if his first cut had been good enough. It didn't budge; we weren't in yet.

"Four minutes before abort," reported the Lieutenant. This was going to be close.

I glanced up and saw a man run up to the smashed window at the front of the bridge. He was hard to make out but he had a knife. A second later, there was a yell, then a loud bang. I rushed to look over the bridge wing. Mike was flat on the deck a long way down. He wasn't moving. His rope was tangled on top of him. *Fucking hell, did that bastard cut the rope?* Keg looked down at Mike, then let out a primal scream and swung at the window with his sledgehammer.

"Come on, you shit of a thing!" Crokes screamed, banging his thick shoulder against the door, pieces of red-hot metal falling onto him. I loaded another rod into his cutter, and he started slicing again. Only one hinge left. I hooked my arm through a small side window by the door we were working on, hoping to reach the handle on the off-chance it wasn't locked. Someone wrenched my hand away and struck my arm with something hard and metal. I swung my fist wildly. Then there was a man screaming in Arabic above us; he was holding a bucket in his hand, but my arm was still through the window, fighting off whoever was in there.

Then he turned the bucket over.

A hellish fireball wrapped its arms around Crokes and me, and we were thrown to the deck. Another fireball came at us, and we frantically rolled and patted ourselves down, the smell of singed hair and uniform sharp in the air. It'd all happened so quickly – and what had happened wasn't clear to us yet. I was drenched. I grabbed a handful of my shirt and brought it to my nose. He'd thrown fuel on us. He'd tried to burn us to a cinder. By some miracle, there were flames all around us, but we were no longer on fire ourselves.

"It's fuel!" I cried out to Crokes. "Don't touch the cutter!" His finger was still on the trigger, the tip of the rod alight. If he pressed it, we were gone. For a moment, my whole world came down to the tip of that rod. Not the mission. Not the bigger war I was fighting in. Not everyone I knew or everything I'd ever known. Just that glowing tip. Crokes wrenched the cylinder off his back, and we stamped out the flames around us, kicking out every smouldering piece of steel. Then I reached for my pistol and looked around. I could feel my eyes boiling with hate, my teeth bared. But Bucketman was gone.

"Entry port side," came through our radios. We were in. Crokes and I left our cutting gear behind and raced down the stairs. We ran past Mike's limp body, the medic leaning over him. I gripped my pistol tight, hate pulsing through me. In the dark insides of the ship, I felt my way quickly forward and towards the best place to come face to face again with the bastards that I wanted to hurt: the bridge. I kicked through wooden doors, pushing people out of the way, our guys and smugglers alike. But by the time I reached the bridge, our team already had some of the crew of *Fal 12* pushed up against the wall, screaming at them not to move, shotguns up and ready. I went for the helm, which was spinning loosely, and swung it hard to starboard to bring us towards international waters and to diplomatic safety. But the rudder didn't move – like pumping the brakes on a car and getting no response. I scanned the engine controls and tried to stop everything. Again, nothing.

"At bridge, helm and engine not responding," I reported through my radio. I looked over my shoulder and saw the *Fal 12* crew being handled roughly downstairs to the holding area. Surely, we were out of time. There was silence on the radio, and for a moment my legs tingled with alarm as I wondered why Lieutenant Hughes wasn't responding.

"Roger, Cutter Black stay there," replied Keg. "All others search for secondary steering compartment, fucking quick time."

The crew of *Fal 12* still had control from somewhere else on the ship and we were quickly moving into Iranian waters, if we weren't already in them. Other than the roar of the helicopter, I heard nothing for an eternity. I was by myself on the bridge, my eyes fixed on the ship's course, occasionally glancing around in case someone threw more fuel on me or up at the oil rig that loomed larger on the near horizon. My right hand throbbed with pain after the hit I'd received when I reached through the window, but I gripped my pistol tight with it, and with my left tapped anxiously on the ship's wheel. "Come on!" I yelled, willing the others to find the secondary steering compartment. After everything that had just happened, it would be a disaster to fail now, and I didn't know how we'd get off, even if we wanted to. The port ladder I had climbed had snapped, and if a man had fallen in from the starboard side, that was likely gone, too. The huge oil rig only a few miles ahead and almost directly in front of us was bad news; we needed to get control quickly or we would crash into that, likely killing us and anyone on the rig. The seconds crawled. The oil that had been thrown over me dripped onto the floor, a slippery puddle pooling.

"We have found the steering compartment, coming to starboard now; bridge let me know if she responds," said Keg across the radio. My eyes were glued to the ship's rudder, waiting for any movement at all, my finger on the radio button ready to report in. Then I grunted with relief. It was slow, but it was working.

"This is Cutter Black. We're coming to starboard. Standby for steering instructions."

We had control.

We were turning back into international waters.

We had taken *Fal 12*.

***

The first candle of sun rose up a few hours later to accompany those of the oil rigs. I was still on the bridge, steering the ship in relatively safe circles at slow speed. I clenched my jaw against the icy chill of desert air coming through the smashed bridge windows and squinted into the waking day, scanning the ocean, my eyes heavy after thirty hours without sleep. My pistol was holstered. To my left, the port bridge wing was charred black from our cutter and from the fireball that had so wanted to wrap us up in its deathly hug. The floor was a mosaic of broken glass. Mike's cut rope still swung limply in the breeze. The door we'd failed to slice through was now open. Crokes had got to work on it an hour ago, like he wanted to settle the score with it.

We hadn't talked about the mission, and I knew we probably never would. No-one seemed to talk about anything in this team. I'd followed along with that approach, and even if I had wanted to, I didn't know who would be able to understand any of it. In fact, it was likely that us two dozen sailors and thirty or so smugglers would be the only people who would ever know about the madness of what happened those last few hours on *Fal 12*. On HMAS *Sydney*, the crew barely knew what we'd be up to when we left each night. They'd celebrated the first boarding we had done, but since then, everyone had slipped into a bored malaise as the ship worked as a base for us to fulfil our missions. We would come back from another operation where a bunch of us should have died, and then over dinner the crew would be talking about how much PlayStation they'd played the night before. We were just the guys who kept our gear in the hangar. And beyond that, very few of them seemed to care – about *Fal 12*, about the wider mission, even about the war. About stopping the oil coming out of Iraq. It certainly didn't feel like any of us wanted to die for the cause.

Back home, my parents probably thought of me daily and maybe sent a prayer my way, but then they were getting on with their lives, going to church, staying busy in their work. I figured my friends from school barely thought about me anymore; I'd been away for a year by then. And sadly, there was no girl who waited for my letters or hoped that I was coming home safe. If I died up here, my existence would fade to a pinprick, then to nothing. What a waste of a life. For so long I thought being a fighting man was what I wanted. What I was supposed to do. That this would be the way that I'd do good in the world. But all this, what I was doing up here, wasn't feeling so good anymore.

The still of the morning was broken by the sound of footsteps coming up the steel steps to the bridge. It was Lieutenant Hughes. His slight nod to acknowledge me belied the terror of what he had been through a few hours earlier. He was the man who fell into the water. I broke the usual code of silence and asked him what happened; he was like a big brother to me up here, and we were two of only a handful of officers in the team. He told me, but he was distant, not quite there with me. The boat on the other side of the ship from where I had climbed had been hit by a big bow wave when he was halfway up the ladder. His grappling hook was hooked on a false guardrail, deliberately cut through by the smugglers and when it had given way he'd fallen twenty feet into the dark midnight ocean. He'd sunk quickly with the weight of his gear and weapons and struggled underwater for what was surely the longest minute of his life, tangled up in the straps of his heavy backpack. Despite pulling the tag on his tactical life jacket, it didn't work, and he kept sinking, disoriented, spinning madly in the pitch-black water, trying to find his way up.

He looked me straight in the eye. "I was dead for all money," he told me. "But then I thought about my boy, and that fucking made me go crazy, so I gave it one last shot." There were no tears from him, not even a catch in his voice, just an absent gaze to somewhere else, far away from here. It must have been all numb for him, too. With his last drop of motivation, he had reached for the torch hooked on his thigh holster, turned it on, kicked like a lunatic, and made it to the surface for half a second before going under again. It had been just enough for the bowman on the fast boat to catch sight of him with his night vision goggles. On a dark night, in rough seas, he was a needle in a haystack. But by a huge stroke of luck, they were able to drag him into the boat.

I didn't say a word. I didn't have any to use.

A message came through the radio from a flat, fatigued Keg.

"Sir, they want to pray."

"Can they do it where they are?" came the snappy response from Lieutenant Hughes.

"No, sir. They want to wash their feet and all that and do it up on deck."

"Okay. Sending down some more numbers now. I'll take the bridge. Spud and Crokes heading your way."

I nodded at him, and made my way down, passing the cabin where Mike lay flat on a grimy mattress, his eyes closed. A morphine pen hung from his mouth, no doubt giving him beautifully woozy sucks of relief and a good sign that he was alive. It was strange to see him like this: one of the most capable guys in the team, out of action. Our armour of invincibility felt like it had a big chink taken out of it, and it didn't feel good. I wondered again if we'd all make it home. If I would.

In the dining room, the smugglers sat on the floor under armed guard. I wanted to hate them, these assholes who had tried in so many ways to kill us. I scanned for the one who threw the bucket of fuel on me and Crokes, but I couldn't recognise him. There were twenty or so, a mix of older men from the Middle East and some younger, I guessed from Southern Asia. Their hair was unbrushed. Stubble on their faces. Tired, blank, defeated. There was a pungent scent of body odour, the kind that oozed out with fear and mixed with fuel and burnt metal. The dining area was stark, with just a few tables and chairs pushed into the corner. The crew's handcuffs had all been taken off, but four of our team stood guard with shotguns, making sure no-one had any silly ideas.

Keg signalled for the men to stand up. "Okay, guys. Prayer time."

***

Soon after, our team was relieved. A steaming party took over to sail *Fal 12* down to a holding area. We'd come to learn in briefings that all of these ships we boarded would be processed by the United Nations inspectors, the Iraqis probably taken through a quick trial and then released, the South Asians sent home, and the ship and oil sold. In time I would learn that the proceeds would go to the UN or maybe even to the offshore bank accounts of some of their most corrupt staff, one of them the son of the Secretary-General.

We headed back to *Sydney* by fast boat and arrived to no fanfare. But the Captain came into the hangar as we packed up and cleaned our weapons and told us that the capture of *Fal 12* was likely the biggest in the history of the sanctions. Admirals, prime ministers and presidents were sending messages of commendation.

While I should have felt pride in all this, I couldn't seem to care anymore. Right then I just wanted some sleep, and thinking ahead I just wanted to make it to the end of the deployment alive.

Famished, I headed to the wardroom to see if I could scrounge up some food. It was dark in there, the lights off in between meals. I didn't bother to turn the light on. I was hoping I wouldn't have to talk to anyone. In the fridge was a single plate, and on it a hunk of dry beef and a stale bread roll. There was a note.

Midshipman Tait, I saved you some food. Stay safe, please. – Seaman Phillips.

Seaman Phillips was the officers' steward, there to look after the wardroom. He was gay, perhaps the first openly gay man I'd met in my rather sheltered life to that point. Plate in hand, I walked slowly to the table, a lump in my throat, the maternal kindness of this steward breaking through my fog. His small act of care felt like the best thing that had happened to me in a while. I sat alone in the dark, my jaw aching its way through the tough, dry beef, and looked down at myself. I was wet with the ocean, fuel and blood; mine or someone else's. Then, numb with exhaustion but deeply appreciative of the food, I headed back to my crew mess and, without taking off my gear, crawled into the tight space of my bed and stared at the metal base of the bed above me. I pleaded for sleep, but it wouldn't come; all the nerve endings in my brain were turned up to eleven with the recurring terror of fireballs, men falling from heights, the deadly water and the piercing eyes of those smugglers on *Fal 12* who had tried so hard to kill us.

I wiped my face with my callused hands still doused in oil, trying to clear everything away, but it all came at me even more rapidly, the smell hurtling unwanted fireworks of trauma to the front of my head. I turned over, switched on my torch, reached for my journal and wrote.

Close calls again last night ... Even closer for some of the other lads. Hope I become a father one day, a grandfather, an old man. In fact ... I just want to fucking make it to nineteen.

I stared at the pages and then rested my tormented head down upon them.

- SIX -

A HAND STRETCHED out of the darkness, grabbed my shoulder and shook me hard.

"Spud, you're going back to *Fal 12*. Get your shit ready."

"What? What time is it? The steaming party has it, don't they?" I said, rubbing my eyes, hoping this was a bad dream.

"Eleven hundred. Boat leaves in ten minutes."

They walked away, off to shake another ten or so guys in Black team who were fit enough to head out again. I breathed heavily, still not sure if I'd actually been shaken awake or if my mind was playing tricks on me, muttering obscenities to myself. I was lucky if I'd had ten minutes of sleep, my first in thirty-six hours. In the hangar, it was clear that only half of us were heading back; the others weren't in any state to go back out, and the remaining few drowsily put our gear back on. No-one talked. We didn't check each other's gear. We barely checked ourselves. Our pistols, still loaded from last night, were holstered on our thighs, shotguns slung over shoulders, and we stepped heavily down the ladder, back into the boat. Hurtling across the flat Persian Gulf, the brief came through our earpieces. We were relieving the steaming party that had taken over from us earlier that morning. *Fal 12* was close, HMAS *Sydney* escorting her south, so the transit across was quick. We came up on her port side, right by the bridge wing, the blackened stain of our fireball taunting me.

On board, Crokes and I were put on guard duty and inside the dining area, we were greeted by the smugglers.

"Welcome back, Navy SEALs!" said a voice. None of our team responded; we didn't even look to see who was speaking. "Who was this bullshit people before?" said the same voice. "You treat us with respect. But these bullshit others, they are no good." The team that had relieved us were good people. Skilled sailors. But they had two things against them. First, their officer was female, and it seemed the Iraqi guys were not interested in taking orders from a woman. Second, we had smashed our way into their ship the night before in a flurry of helicopters, guns and sparks. After ten years of attempts from other units, our small team had successfully handled everything they had thrown at us and taken control. We had defeated these guys, and they were impressed.

"Have you eaten yet?" asked Lieutenant Hughes, pointing at an Iraqi smuggler. The smuggler shook his head. "Spud, find the cook and keep a close guard on him while he makes some chow."

The smugglers pointed at a man, and when I motioned to him, he stood up, pulling up his long suit pants, which hung loosely around his waist. He didn't have a belt, and his tan singlet was splotched with stains. He was heavyset, probably Iraqi, and looked to be in his fifties, with a bald head pocked with sunspots, a shoe polish–like smear of stubble on his wrinkled brown face, and scarred, thick hands. I was dressed in my tactical gear, 160 pounds of wiry muscle, a shaved head and two days' stubble on my face. My hands weren't as big as his, but I had a gun that I was happy to use if he tried anything. We made our way through the old, smashed-up ship towards the galley, some of the damage no doubt from our team. I kept two metres between us, scanning the way ahead for threats, my hand down loose, opening and closing near my pistol.

He got to work in silence, measuring cups of flour from a plastic tub and pouring them into a scratched bucket. Taking a cup of dirty oil from a grimy bottle. The storage shelves were mostly empty, save for a few sacks of flour, some teabags, sugar and salt. The old stovetops were rusted over and looked like they hadn't been used in a while, a small gas cooker on the floor in the centre of the room favoured by the cook. I made a quick sweep around the space, securing any knives away on a top shelf, and then stood in the doorway, watching his every move. A dull pulse thudded away behind my eyes, and it felt like my balance kept swinging from my forehead to the base of my skull.

"You must be tired. You should sit," he said to me after a few minutes, moving an old wooden stool into the middle of the kitchen and reaching in for a handful of flour.

I shook my head. I wasn't in the mood for smuggler tricks.

"This food will take some time. Maybe hour. You should sit," he said again, motioning again towards the chair.

"No," I replied, a little too loudly. I stayed firm, my hands clasped in front of me in the security pose we'd been trained to hold, careful to keep a few metres between us.

"Okay," he said, putting his dry palms out in defeat, white flour puffing up into the air as he did.

I watched in silence as he sat on a short stool, patiently and deliberately mixing flour with water in an old plastic tub and kneading the dough with his leathered hands. Twenty or so minutes passed like this, a tray of dough balls piling up. Then he motioned again for me to sit.

I was exhausted. His eyes were honest. I didn't think he was going to try to trick or attack me.

Bugger it. I'd sit.

I sat on the wooden stool and looked at him, adjusting my pistol in its holster to remind him that I was still in charge here. He saw my show of bravado and smiled. "This takes a long time," he repeated as he handed me a ball of dough. "Maybe it will be quicker if you help. I make tea for us." I took the ball and started working it around in my hand, the stickier bits clumping on my fingers. He pinched some flour from the bucket and sprinkled it over my hands and then stood to light the gas cooker and set some water to boil. I continued to watch him closely, still waiting for an attack of some kind. But we just sat in silence. Rolling dough. Not looking at each other. I glanced from his hands down to the balls of dough in mine, back to his. I kept scanning the room. I felt like I'd broken some rules here – I'd put myself at risk. Then the water was boiled, and he got up to make tea. Black with lots of sugar. I was still on edge; a boiling pot was certainly a weapon if he wanted it to be. But he was whistling a tune as he poured out two cups, and then he passed me a mug, the handle broken off. The mug was hot against my palms. He sat back down on his stool, took a sip of tea and grabbed another handful of dough.

We'd been briefed to never take anything offered by the smugglers in case it was poisoned. But I'd seen him make everything, he'd taken a sip right in front of me, and a cup of tea would do wonders for my weary bones. I took a drink. The warm, sweet liquid relaxed me, and maybe it was just the exhaustion, but for a second, I mistook him for my beloved grandfather, an Austrian migrant who had fled post-war Europe. I shook away the mirage.

"You very good last night, you Navy SEALs." He smiled at me, with only a smattering of yellow teeth remaining in his gums. "We tried to stop you good, but you were too strong. Very good, you Navy SEALs," he said and nodded.

"I'm not a Navy SEAL," I said, lifting up the Velcro patch on my shoulder to expose the Australian flag to him. "Australian."

"I know," he laughed, which gave way to a racking, rattling cough. "If you were American, we are dead now!" Then he used his finger to make a gun, which he pointed at his head.

I sighed and shrugged.

"What is your name?" I asked, reaching for another handful of dough. Maybe I could get some intelligence and pass it back to Lieutenant Hughes.

"Farooq," he said, touching his chest, then pointed to me.

We'd been told not to give out our names, and we wore no ranks or identification on our uniforms. You didn't want to become a target for terrorists, the intelligence team had said. Your families would be put in danger, they had warned us. But this was the first time since I'd been in the Gulf that I'd actually talked with a smuggler, aside from screaming at them to "get down" in the few heated minutes of each boarding. I'd already broken a lot of rules in this kitchen, but Farooq didn't seem like the kind of guy who was going to have Al Qaeda come and murder my family. Maybe we were just two human beings, an old man and a young one, making bread together.

"Aaron."

"What does 'Aaron' mean?" he asked.

"Not sure, actually. What does 'Farooq' mean?"

"It means one who speaks the truth," he said, looking straight into my eyes.

"Nice name," I nodded, and grabbed a handful of dough. "What is it like in Iraq now?"

"Oh, Iraq is very difficult," he replied, shaking his head.

"Is it because of Saddam?" I placed a completed ball of dough on the bench.

"Yes, maybe some is Saddam, but mostly is because of this UN sanction. Is very tough. No money, no medicine, no food, no water, no job. So I take this job on ship." He picked up the tray of dough and moved over to the cooker to start firing the flatbreads.

"Do you have family in Iraq?" I asked.

"Yes. Of course. I am old man. I am blessed with two boys and one daughter. Five grandchildren. Some have died. I have not seen others in long time. Maybe now I don't see them again. What will happen to us, Mr Aaron?"

"I don't know, Farooq." We looked at each other. Then he looked down and put the first ball of dough onto the charred frying pan, flattening it with his palm.

And I really didn't know.

I was eighteen years old. I had no idea what was happening two ranks above me, let alone what decisions were being made at the United Nations headquarters in New York. I would later come to learn that Farooq, the man sitting opposite me, sharing his tea with me, talking about his family, rolling balls of dough, was just a number. The *Fal 12* boarding would be entered into a UN spreadsheet with different columns for each piece of data.

Number of men arrested
Barrels of oil seized
Smugglers' lives lost
Injuries and deaths of boarding team sailors and officers

While those numbers were added to the tally, UN workers would take long lunches in expensive restaurants in midtown New York. The American government would hold firm on the sanctions, veto any attempt to have them repealed by the Security Council, and secretly prepare for a full land invasion of Iraq and decades of war. We would all keep hunting for the terrorists. A handful of corrupt officials assigned to the sanctions would become rich, skimming money illegally from the takings of the seized oil. Academics from universities in cold cities in England and America would write journal articles about the sanctions, but these would go largely unread. My boarding team would return home broken and never speak of these missions again. Some of the guys would kill themselves. But there would be another team ready to take our place – in fact, my older brother Michael would be in one of them, and I wouldn't even speak of this mission with him or hear about his. The history wouldn't be spoken of, perhaps out of fatigue, or maybe even out of shame. I kept thinking that it was all for nothing. All this suffering, for nothing. And I thought that while perhaps there were "just" wars, and maybe one day I'd fight in one, to me, sitting there that day with Farooq, nothing felt just. Or good.

And through all of this, Farooq and his family would struggle on. Or maybe they would die too.

***

"Flying Stations close up. Standby to receive Desert Duck. Midshipman Tait, Captain's cabin."

The Desert Duck was the American Navy helicopter that came to our ship a few times a week to drop off supplies, pick up any injured and conduct transfers across the units of the Persian Gulf. That day it was there for me, and it would take me to Bahrain, where I would board a flight back to Australia. My first year in the military had come to an end, and I was returning to begin my university and officer studies at the Academy. I would be reuniting with my officers' class and my best mates, Kel and Apples. While Army and Air Force officers started at the Academy straight from high school, we were starting as navy divers, with active service, war medals on our chest and, based on some rumours swirling, a bravery citation along with the rest of the team for the *Fal 12* boarding. The mission had broken the back of the smuggler network – ever since that day, boardings had been less frequent and far easier, almost entirely on smaller boats with no booby traps. HMAS *Sydney* and the rest of the boarding team would stay on in the Gulf for a little while longer before taking a slow, circuitous route home to Australia, with a few port visits for the crew to let off some steam in the bars and brothels of Southeast Asia.

I hurtled up the steps to the captain's cabin and knocked sharply, knowing that the Desert Duck would be landing in only a few minutes. "Come in!"

I entered and stood in front of the captain's desk. His cabin was huge. Wall-to-wall redwood. Dark green carpet. He looked up from his papers. He was a short man in his fifties, with a full head of black hair and thin glasses on his intelligent face. A quiet, methodical officer who liked to keep to himself, he was highly respected by the crew. Much of this respect came down to the deep care he seemed to hold for all of us; he knew our names, checked on us after missions, and made decisions to keep us safe as we faced danger. We had chatted a handful of times during the deployment. The first was when I had cut the ship's cake with him on Christmas Day, fulfilling tradition as the youngest member of the crew. As we had posed for a photo, the alarm had sounded for the boarding team to move out, cutting our conversation short. "Merry Christmas," he'd said with a smile as I'd excused myself.

He put down his pen, blew out a sharp breath, and then spoke. "Midshipman Tait, before you leave, I just wanted to tell you that I think you have a big life ahead of you. You've performed well beyond your years up here and impressed many sailors and officers on board. I am proud of you."

"Thank you, sir." I nodded, pride surging through my body.

"I would gladly serve with you again."

"It's been an honour to serve under your command, sir." It felt good to be recognised as a capable young officer by this older man of the sea. For a moment, a little part of me wanted to not board the chopper, to stay with the men, keep proving myself, keep fighting.

"Now get down to that hangar; I can hear the Desert Duck coming," he said and motioned with his hand.

I thanked him and raced through the huge grey ship, home to 220 sailors and officers, yelling goodbye to as many of them as I could on my way. I zigzagged through the busiest sections to try to catch people who had become like family, past the black operations room lit up with hundreds of lights from radar and satellite displays. Past the officers' mess with its wood-panelled walls and brass fittings, through the sailors' mess with swimsuit magazines resting on plastic tables. Down the corridors crowded with pipes, firefighting equipment and weapons and into the ship's helicopter hangar. Black boarding team were cleaning their weapons. These were good, proud men, and I felt honoured to have been a part of their team.

I looked Crokes in the eye and shook his hand. He nodded; and with no words, all was said.

I owed him my life, and I'd never see him again. I'd never have the chance to thank him for reaching over and holding me from falling to my death as that ladder had broken. Maybe I'd saved his life when that fireball had come for us, and I'd smelled the fuel. A thousand maybes, a thousand thank-yous. All unsaid.

This team would never work together as a unit again; and indeed, over the rest of my career I would only bump into these individuals occasionally, in the dark night of an exercise or at the local bar on Veteran's Day. Each time, no-one would ever speak about this deployment. Some of the guys would become alcoholics. Many of the married guys would divorce. Some would kill themselves. But for now, for this short moment, there was a warmth, a respect, a brotherhood. I was the youngest brother, but maybe I had held my own as a warrior.

I stepped out onto the flight deck, ducked low under the roaring rotors of the chopper, grabbed a metal handle and pulled myself inside, my two bags already stowed by the air crew. I sat down on a hard webbing seat, closed my eyes and took a deep breath. I'd made it out. I'd have the chance to live my life, rather than seeing it snuffed out on an oily smuggling ship in the Persian Gulf. I knew I had to make the most of what I'd been given.

Then we lifted off, the helicopter shaking violently as the pilot brought on the power. We circled low around the ship, past the port bridge wing and off towards the hazy horizon in the direction of Manama City. I didn't have a radio, and the American crew had things to do, so I sat alone with my thoughts.

I thought about kissing my mother goodbye on the cheek a year earlier, telling her I would leave home as a boy and come back one day as a man. It had happened quicker than I had expected; the boy was gone, replaced by a gnarlier, meaner version on his way to being a man, scarred both outside and in.

I had grown up wanting to be a fighter, in the tradition of the men in my family, and straight out of high school I had been given a front-row seat to the War on Terror. But now, as I flew away from this mission, I was confused. Was this mission right? Was being a professional fighter the way I would exist in this world? I had proven myself, but in the process, I had almost lost more lives than an eighteen-year-old should. Could I see myself coming up here and doing all this again? Did I really want to become a fully qualified Special Forces soldier and fight in even more aggressive missions? There were plenty of genuinely bad guys out there who were worth the scrap. But for every one of them, how many Farooqs were there?

I didn't know who to talk to about all this. There was no debriefing and no psychologist coming to speak with me. My parents would probably want to talk about what I should do with the $15,000 I had saved up here and what smart financial decisions I could make. My schoolmates were on a different planet from me now; they wouldn't understand. I wouldn't have a girlfriend giving me a kiss when I landed. I felt so alone. I didn't know where I wanted to be, but it wasn't here anymore. The chopper banked to the right and dipped down low over the ocean, every wop of its blades taking me farther away from war.

PART 2

ESCAPE

- SEVEN -

THE WILD TURBULENCE that buffeted the plane as it neared Perth Airport was soothed by the free rum I had been drinking since we'd left Singapore. I was coming home. Home to a place that I'd left more than a year before. Home to a family that loved me, and friends I'd graduated from high school with. I felt ready to feel loved and supported by my parents, to sleep soundly and to maybe come out of this fog I'd felt trapped in. As the seatbelt sign turned off I stood up, the left knee I'd injured on dive course throbbing. I reached up for my small backpack, a salt-stained and weathered black tactical bag that seventy-two hours earlier had held my weapons. Now it was almost empty, with my journal, my civilian and military passports, and my wallet with my probationary driver's license and bank card. In the hold below were the rest of my possessions, now down to one bag that held my diving wetsuits, my boarding kit, two changes of civilian clothes and my knife.

I moved through immigration, and my bag passed customs quickly with a nod from an airport officer wearing medals on his chest that showed he was a veteran himself. Then I stepped out into Australia and saw Mum. She was wearing blue jeans and a grey motorcycle t-shirt, a hobby they'd got into recently. I figured Dad was doing laps with the car, not wanting to pay for the parking fee. I walked right up to her, my backpack on my left shoulder and my green canvas bag on my right. It felt nice to see her, comforting. Like she was the only person in the world who would be able to wrap me up in a hug, not ask me what I'd been through, just cook my favourite meal and offer to do my washing for me. But she looked straight past me, over my shoulder, hoping to spot her son. Me.

"Mum, it's me," I said quietly with a small laugh.

She pushed my arm to the side, craning into the crowd as passengers streamed out of customs. I put my bags down and put a hand on each of her shoulders.

"Mum, it's Aaron. I'm right here."

Her head kicked back just an inch, shocked by this brutish stranger in front of her. My hair was shaved short, my skin deeply tanned and leathery, my eyes sunken with fatigue. Twenty pounds of new muscle on the skinny boy she'd said goodbye to the year before. That boy was long gone.

"Oh, Aaron, gosh, oh give me a hug," she said and laughed thinly.

I reached down to the barely five feet of her, a proud, strong Austrian migrant, and gave her a hug. She told me that we had to hurry, that Dad was in the car doing the loops of the airport, as I'd expected.

I stayed for three days, but the fog didn't lift as I had hoped. My parents were loving and supportive. Mum washed my clothes and made me spaghetti bolognese, but once that was done, we hardly knew what to talk about. Dad was busy with work. My younger brother Daniel was pleasantly oblivious to what I'd been up to and spent those three days doing what fourteen-year-olds should be doing: cycling around the neighborhood, flirting with girls and swimming at the beach. Out of politeness I went along to church, and the pastor even asked me to come on stage, interviewing me about my time away. When he asked me how Jesus had helped me in the Middle East, I lied and told the congregation it was prayer that got me through, both mine and theirs. They lovingly prayed for me again, reaching out their hands to bless me.

I texted my friends from school, suggesting we catch up at the pub for a beer, but they asked if we could meet at the food hall instead; they'd signed an agreement at church saying they wouldn't step inside a bar or casino as youth leaders. Which was fine, and something I might have done had I not joined the military. They were wonderfully consistent with who they had been when I'd left. It was me that had changed.

Home wasn't home anymore.

***

It felt good to get back on a plane. To escape again. And after a flight across Australia, I landed in Canberra, the national capital and home to the Defence Force Academy, where I was set to spend the next three years. Apples and Kel had already arrived, and they'd picked up my room key for me, but I'd also be reuniting with my classmates from basic training. Most had nicknames. Smooch was a feisty but loving lesbian from Brisbane. Noodles, an opinionated and tall rugby player who was said to be "done in two minutes" in the bedroom. Shitters, a nuggety farmer from Queensland, had had a toilet explode over him in the Solomon Islands. Two Dads was a whip-smart girl from Sydney who simply had a hyphenated surname, while Spoons wasn't as sharp as a knife. Stretch was too tall for his reflexes to keep up, and Stubbsy was a compact ball of muscle and a star football player. A posh girl from Melbourne with the surname Higgins was turned into Henry after the *My Fair Lady* character. Trent didn't have a nickname, but was the happiest guy in every bar, usually with a drink in each hand, one for him and one for you. He was a music fan, and we'd stayed up late in basic training many nights listening to Bob Dylan, The Doors and Pink Floyd.

I was impressed as the taxi drove me down the hill and pulled up to the main roundabout of the Academy. The manicured gardens, modern buildings and water fountains were a long way from the stoic buildings of the dive school, or the oil-slicked decks of HMAS *Sydney*. I looked up at the flags of the Air Force, Army and Navy, cracking proudly in the sharp breeze. At the Academy, all three services trained together, but the Navy took a slightly different approach. While the first-year Army and Air Force cadets had just graduated from high school, Navy officers were sent to the Navy Officer school in remote Jervis Bay for initial training, and then out to the fleet for the second half of the year. The Admirals wanted to see if we were tough enough to survive out in the fleet before they invested a million dollars in each of us to put us through the Academy. We were arriving to the Academy not as cadets like the others, but as commissioned officers with an overinflated chip on our shoulders, a love of a drink, a low threshold for a fight and, for some of us, medals and trauma from the missions we'd just served on. But now three years of leadership training and university studies awaited us. It felt new and exciting, and I was happy to start studying. I'd done well in high school, was fascinated by economics, history, politics and literature, and this was a place I could indulge in books while also being paid $18,000 a year.

I found my way to our block, the accommodation building that housed thirty of us, and then to my own room, on the second floor. I dropped my bags and sat on the single bed to take in my new home: a small heater, a wooden desk and a bookshelf. In the window outside was a chin-up bar, a place I knew Kel, Apples and I would spend time each night to stay in shape for the diving unit. Ten, then nine, then eight, all the way down to one each night before dinner. It was also a good time to talk, as we waited our turn on the bar.

And then they both walked into my room. They'd coordinated things so we were all on the same floor. Kel was barefoot, wearing board shorts and no t-shirt, tanned from a few weeks surfing after he'd returned home from the Gulf. Breaking the rules already of no alcohol in the accommodation, he held three open beers in his hands and passed one to me with a nod. I knew he'd had a rough time of it up in the Persian Gulf, while I'd been there, too; they'd been captured during a covert mission to an unnamed country, but had managed, by some miracle, to escape. Apples, dressed in running gear, was slick with sweat after jogging a few miles in the summer sun. They both looked fit and healthy, but I wondered how their minds were, if they were anything like mine: confused, busy, wound up like a spring. But we didn't go there, maybe we didn't need to yet. It felt good to be together.

***

As the opening piano bars of "Khe Sanh" boomed across the speakers, Stubbsy, always surprisingly agile for a man with so much muscle, was up on the wooden bar as quick as a flash, a handful of plastic straws in his fist serving as a makeshift microphone. The carpet was sticky with a million spills and discarded pieces of gum, and the lighting too dark to make out which banknotes were in your wallet. The name gave it away; O'Malley's was Irish-themed, with the requisite dusty typewriters, the cheapest vintage books and out of context black-and-white photos sent over from Dublin. Since arriving at the Academy, we had decided this was our place. The goals here were drunkenness and a good time and while the bouncers hated us, the bargirls pretended to love us. The only sure thing with O'Malley's was a hangover.

Apples and I were leaning against the bar, sneaking glances at two blondes who sat at a nearby table as they played with the straws in their gin and tonics. But our conversation was less light-hearted than it might have seemed. While Kel and I had been in the Middle East, Apples had been in the Timor Sea, enforcing Australia's incredibly tight and often inhumane "Stop the Boats" policy. How this played out in the open ocean was that our navy would board refugee vessels, turn them back towards Indonesia and give them just enough fuel to make it back to the coast. The boats, often dangerously overcrowded and unseaworthy, sometimes never made it to shore. Apples had been in the thick of much of it, and it was clear as he talked about it tonight that he was as conflicted about this as I was about what I had been doing off the coast of Iraq. Stubbsy held his own on the bar top, fending off a security guard with his free hand and trying to close out the song. Apples was opening up to me for the first time. The booze seemed to be helping.

"This one Indonesian sailor was pleading with us, saying that if we left the boat, he would be killed by the refugees," he said, looking past me into the crowd. Apples didn't look sad, just distant. The same way I felt. But there was an anger in him. His lips were thin. Eyes narrow. "As we moved away and the refugees realised what was happening, I saw them run towards him and the crew and begin attacking them. We just turned and left, but later that day a big storm rolled in. I don't reckon they made it. But it all happened so fast; the orders had to have been coming from people well above our Captain."

It was rare for us to talk about what we'd been through. We had been offered no counselling or psychological support, and we knew that we were way too low down the pecking order to even think about publicly challenging the missions we'd been part of. But tonight, we were voicing the questions that went through our heads when we tried to sleep. With a school principal as his mother, and a school groundsman as his father, Apples matched a fierce intelligence with a distrust for authority, so he had been doing his own research into the border policies, as I had been questioning the Iraq sanctions. With a face like Will Hunting and a similar knack for finding his way into a fight, he was both a good and bad guy to have as a best mate.

Trent danced his way towards us, an unlit cigarette hanging lazily from his mouth and a drinks tray crowded with beers and glasses of Kahlua and Coke in one hand.

By now, Stubbsy had been pulled off the bar, and four bouncers, knowing how he always loved a scrap, had him by each limb. The jangly riffs of "Eagle Rock" by Daddy Cool started up, which in this bar meant only one thing: pants down and drink up. Trent placed the drinks tray on the bar next to us, pulled his pants down – ours too – and snapped us out of our chat.

"Oh, cheer up, you sad, sad bastards," he said with a slur. We sang along to "Eagle Rock", drank our lagers down to halfway, then poured in the Coke and Kahlua to make our crew's special mix, the Bertie Beatle, so named as it tasted like a candy bar we'd all grown up eating at the Easter Show. A guaranteed hangover. With another few mouthfuls, they were drained, and with an inviting wave from the two blondes, we headed towards the dance floor, pulling up our pants as we went. But before the song finished, we were out on the street, led out the same door they had just thrown Stubbsy through. One of us had upset the bouncers, though it was a blur as to who.

On the street, there was the regular chorus of chatting, breaking glass and police sirens as well as the usual cologne of Saturday night – urine, beer, cigarettes and spices from the chicken shop. For a few minutes we made our own contributions to the aroma, decided against an offered-up fight with someone we didn't know, tried to pick one with some guys we did, and then we were falling into a taxi. Inside, we were loud and there were too many of us for the seats available, but the driver was a good sport or just couldn't be bothered to protest, and he turned up the radio and drove into the night.

We passed the crowd outside O'Malley's, cheering our mates and giving the finger to those who weren't. Apples passed around a paper box of fries, and driving past the National War Memorial a few minutes later, we gave a salty-fingered salute to those who had fallen. Trent slurred along to the song on the radio, his hands conducting the beat limply and his head rolled back. A few minutes later, we came down the hill to the Academy, and I knew that if we kept up this behaviour, we would almost certainly get into some trouble on base and likely secure ourselves another round of punishments – we had already spent plenty of weekends painting rocks in the sun. I patted my pockets for coins to chip in for the fare and then we stepped out of the taxi, the officers' mess lit up like a castle. We were young, laughing and, for a moment, drunk enough to forget all the heavy ideas we had been working through as young officers. We stumbled away from the taxi, ready for a few pints of water, and a broken sleep.

"Where's Trent?" someone asked.

He replied with one word and a wave goodbye. "Seeya!" We all looked around at him. He was sitting on the back of the taxi, which for a moment was funny. His kind of joke. The driver didn't know he was there, though, and he started to drive away quickly, eager to collect another fare before the bars closed. Trent held on, his legs kicking up into the air as the cab accelerated, but as it headed towards the hill, he jumped off.

His head hit the road with a sickening thud, the taxi fading away into the distance.

Apples and I ran to him as fast as we could, and as we skidded in alongside his body, there was already blood oozing from his head, the puddle spreading. It was thick. Dark. There was too much life pouring out of him. I tried to hold my hand to where it was all coming from, but it was warm, wet, sticky, horrifying. He murmured something unintelligible, but there was too much blood coming out of his mouth.

"You're okay, mate," I said, a little too high-pitched, a little too loud. We laid him flat. "You're okay, mate."

"Call an ambulance!" Apples yelled back to the rest of the group who had just caught up. "And run to the base hospital as fast as you can, see if they have anyone on duty." Trent was limp already, his eyes rolled back in his head. His throat gurgled, and hellish red bubbles popped up from between his teeth as we rolled him into the recovery position. He was unconscious, with the smallest hint of pulse and breath. Time never goes as slowly as when you are waiting for an ambulance and I glanced up at the hill, willing the blue and red lights to arrive.

Apples and I cradled his head to keep him out of his own blood and I wiped it away from his mouth with my shirt. We held his hands, rubbing his with our thumbs like worried parents with a feverish child. We talked to him, told him that we were with him. But he was leaving us. The ambulance arrived, and it was a blur of flashing lights, plastic wrappers and rubber tubes. The paramedics moved quickly enough, but it seemed like they knew.

- EIGHT -

I AWOKE FROM a nightmare, breathing heavily through my nose, my hands grasping at my mouth. I'd been underwater on a dive. It had been at night, in the Gulf and I'd been under a ship. I was hooked on something and couldn't see or feel what was keeping me stuck, but my tank was running out, and each time I sucked on my regulator I was getting a smaller and smaller sip of air. I rubbed my eyes aggressively with my palms and then looked around, trying to figure out where I was. Apples was curled up next to me on a hard plastic chair. I looked down at myself, my shirt covered with blood.

We were at the hospital. And if we were still here, maybe Trent was still alive. We'd called the on-duty officer at the Academy to tell him about what had happened and then the two of us had got a taxi to try to find out where they had taken Trent. The Academy had been in touch with his mother who lived in the next state and was already on her way. We hadn't seen him yet, but a kind doctor told us he'd been in surgery for hours as they'd cut open his skull and worked to reduce the massive swelling in his brain. I left Apples to get some more sleep and headed outside for some sun. It was late in the morning, but the day was dull and grey. I spotted a sickly man dressed in a hospital gown, his legs dark and veined and his thin wrist shaking as he drew a dying cigarette up to his dying lips. He cupped it in the military fashion shielding it from the wind and hiding it from the enemy. I motioned to my lips with two fingers and his head lifted an inch and he passed me the packet in his other hand. I thanked him and struck open the zippo lighter, marked with the shield of an army unit. I flicked it once, twice, three times and it gave a lick of flame, the cigarette crackling softly as I took three draws. The nicotine gave me a momentary lapse of reality, and I closed my eyes to try to forget both what had happened the night before and what was happening now. I wondered who would come to visit Trent. His mum certainly, but who else cared for him? Who would miss him if he didn't make it? Apples and I were friends with him, but not that close. Certainly not close enough to be the only ones here if he wasn't going to make it.

Then his mother arrived. Fran. I recognised her from graduation night of basic training. She'd been so proud of her boy, a working-class lad from a public high school wearing the crisp white uniform of a naval officer, his ceremonial sword at his waist. I went over to her and wrapped my arm around her shoulder. Her hair was wild; she'd obviously got straight out of bed and driven immediately to the airport, not even packing a bag. I told her I would take her to where he was, and she whimpered a response, panic pouring from every pore.

As we walked into the intensive care unit, I talked quietly to the nurse at the desk while Fran gripped my hand tightly. "We are here to see Trent Norton. He was admitted last night; this is his mother, Fran."

As were led into the room, the line that got me through missions in Iraq circled through my head: *Be strong and take heart, be strong and take heart.* I had to be strong for Fran, but in those first seconds all of the strength I was trying to muster was for nothing. He was a mess. She made an otherworldly noise as she collapsed onto him, a long guttural moan surging up from the depths of her. Her universe, her beautiful boy, had tubes coming out of his mouth, his heart and his wrists. Bloodied bandages were wrapped around his head. His eyes were closed, but black and swollen. Pumps hissed with air and monitors beeped slowly, the machines that were keeping him alive.

But not for long.

He died later that night, and his funeral was later that week.

We wore our ceremonial uniforms and carried his coffin. The prime minister said a few words, more than we did. I was asked to give the speech on behalf of us officers, surprised that it was me who was selected, and wondering if someone else was closer to him. More appropriate. I looked around the people at the ceremony and recognised only his family and our classmates. We made weak small talk at the wake, trying to work our way through tasteless sandwiches cut into triangles. I couldn't eat, the lump of emotion in my throat too thick, and I put down my creased paper plate to hug Trent's mum as she walked by. She didn't want to let go, and I made sure I wasn't the first to.

After it all, I changed into warm clothes and headed out into dusk for a run into the nearby national park. Kel and Apples came as well, and still nothing was said. We jogged until we found a hill, where I quietly started to make a small cairn of rocks. The others joined in, and with a pile of rocks two feet high, we sat back and looked out over the valley. "Trent's hill," I said. The other two just nodded, swallowing down their emotion like the men we had been conditioned to be.

***

Kel, Apples, and I found ourselves making this evening run through the national park a habit. We would run late into the night, returning to our room for a few hours of sleep before carrying on with our full day of officer training and studies.

We started going out for thirty-six-hour stretches over the weekends of nonstop running, cycling, kayaking and late-night abseils from remote clifftops. Our pain, sleep deprivation, blistered feet and exhausted bodies served to distract us from Trent's death and everything else we should have been trying to work through. If we were too exhausted to talk, it meant we didn't have to.

But we also drank. Sometimes, I drank so much that I let my emotions roar out of me after I'd snuck out of the bar and stumbled home in the freezing cold, my jacket pulled in tight around my body. Sometimes, I didn't get out of the bar in time, and that emotion was directed towards someone else with my fists. I was fighting too much. I was angry. I was not good.

After the first half of the year at the Academy, two things had become clear.

Firstly, my attitude towards being in the military was changing.

I had been so excited as a high-school student when I had opened my letter of offer, but now the thought of being at the Academy for two more years and serving out my total service obligation of seven made my chest tight with anxiety. The contract I had signed as a seventeen-year-old felt like a prison sentence. Making it worse were the constant reminders from senior officers that if we decided to quit now, there would be an accompanying bill for a few hundred thousand dollars to reimburse the training that the government had invested in us. I was trapped.

In my first semester, I had been motivated to excel, just like I had with the diving and boarding teams. I had won the award for the best academic and leadership performance in my unit, but after Trent's death, I had begun to disengage. Perhaps it was because I couldn't get my head straight as I waded through the shock and sadness of his death. Trent had died so suddenly, falling off the back of a taxi after a drunken night out. For all the things I'd survived since I'd joined the military, I couldn't understand why he'd died the way he did. He was there, sitting in the taxi with us and then he was gone.

But another thought had started to gnaw its way into my head, and I didn't know how to talk about it with anyone. When he had first died, everyone was sad. There were tears, drunken singalongs and beers poured to the ground in his honor. But then everyone moved on. The next week there were rugby games to be played. Happy hours at O'Malley's. Boots to be polished and uniforms to be ironed. We all just forgot.

His mother would mourn him for the rest of her life, and we knew of one of his school friends who studied locally that we would raise a glass to if we saw her at the bar. But beyond that, we all just got on with it.

The thought of dying like that, of being forgotten so quickly... well, it terrified me. It was a selfish, shocking thought, but I had this desperate need to live a bigger life. To love deeply and be loved deeply in return. To travel the world and live a life of great adventure. To make a difference to someone, or many people, somewhere in the world. To have lived. To have mattered, if only for a moment.

The trouble was, living a life like that... I just couldn't see it happening in the military.

***

I clicked on the Word document on my screen, titled "Politics Paper 2", and stared at the question in bold type across the top.

> **Detail the greatest strategic military threat to Australia – 4000 words.**

The words blurred; I sighed and ran my hands, callused from the gym, across my hair, which I had been instructed to cut short the day before. My essay's introduction accounted for 128 words so far; only 3,872 to go. But I couldn't think of what to write, and if I was honest with myself, I was finding it hard to be inspired by the question.

I glanced at the time in the top corner of the screen: 11:50pm. In six hours, the on-duty officer would sound the wake-up call for the day, and we would have marching practice for an upcoming military parade, followed by shooting practice, a schedule of academic classes, and then a few hours of cleaning before an evening inspection of our barracks. My small room was a mess, and notes, journal articles and library books were strewn across both the bed and floor. By the door were my muddy running shoes. Hanging from the back of my door was a tattered white-and-red signal flag, a memento of the *Fal 12* boarding that I had snuck into my backpack and brought home with me. It was the only reminder I allowed of that time.

I leaned back in my government-issued chair and took a swig of wine. We'd been caught with alcohol in our barracks twice already by the instructors, the biggest punishment coming when they discovered the six-gallon barrel of beer we'd been brewing. But I had found that a half dozen $2 bottles of red a week from the liquor store in town were helping me get through the frustration of being at the Academy and worth the risk.

I reached across to my bed and picked up a thick academic article that I had printed at the library, detailing the latest military acquisitions by the Indonesian government, hoping to read about the new weapon they were developing that would classify as the "greatest strategic military threat to Australia" and give me the answer for my essay. I scanned the first page and after a minute dropped the document to the floor. I reached across again to pick up another printout, this one an Oxfam report on the impacts in India of an innovative economics concept called microfinance. I read on about a man from nearby Bangladesh called Muhammad Yunus, a professor who had used his university-taught knowledge to open banks for the poor. I could picture myself doing this kind of work one day, in foreign places all around the world. It felt like a version of doing good that aligned with my growing interest in economics and global politics.

In military strategy lectures, I had begun hiding reports like this Oxfam one, reading them while I pretended to listen to battlefield tactics. In economics classes, I half listened to theories and graphs designed for Western economies while I wondered whether these really applied across Africa, Asia, Latin America. In politics lectures, I put asterisks and exclamations alongside paragraphs about military interventions, asking myself why Gulf War One would have so many foreign troops engaged, but Rwanda could experience a genocide with almost complete inaction. But I knew the answer. There was no oil in Rwanda.

After flicking through the Oxfam report, I took another swig of red wine, and an idea started to take shape in my mind. At the end of the year, I had Christmas leave. I knew I needed to get away from the military and I also knew that spending my leave at home with my parents and their sincere requests for me to come to church didn't feel right. I needed to go somewhere where no-one knew who I was, or who I had been. I wanted to go to India, to see what this place was really like. To see if I was as excited there as I was reading these reports.

And if there was one person I might know who would want to come with me, it was Apples, someone who was struggling with the military as much as I was, and who was always happy, if he was sober, to talk about the problems of the world with an earnestness that matched mine. His older brother, a successful actor who was more progressive than we were, had been challenging his thinking about his role in the border patrols, as well as Australia's support of the treatment of prisoners by the Americans at Guantanamo Bay.

I mashed the keyboard of my computer to light up the screen and typed a short note to him on Instant Messenger. He responded immediately, no doubt up working late on the same military strategy paper.

Hey mate, I've got an idea for you, I typed onto the screen and pressed enter.

He responded quickly.

Shoot. Anything to get me away from this bloody paper.

Let's travel around India over the Christmas holidays … Should be a good adventure and I really want to get away from Australia … I am reading about this micro-finance idea super interesting. Maybe one day we can use these economics degrees of ours for something useful. You in?

I pressed enter and waited for his response, taking the last swig of wine from the bottle, a grainy mouthful of sediment sliding roughly down my throat.

Maybe … wait, I'll come over.

Two minutes later, he opened my door and walked in with a map of India, which smelled like it had come straight from the printer. He was dressed in a thick woollen jumper hand-knitted by his Tasmanian mother and had half a bottle of our trusty $2 red in one hand.

By 3am, we had planned a rough route around the country, sketched out with an HB pencil. Starting in New Delhi on Christmas Day, we would travel by third-class sleeper trains around the country. It was to be a boy's adventure, and another journey to a land foreign to our own. It was also an escape, somewhere far, far away from the Academy. And I had an unscratched itch. A small but growing compassion for the lives of people living in extreme poverty. And a curiosity if there was anything I could personally do about it.

I couldn't wait.

- NINE -

With our train not leaving for a few hours, Apples and I sat on our bags at Delhi station, the central travel hub for a city of 33 million people. An endless caravan of travellers zigzagged through the main hall, families heading home and workers crossing the country, everyone moving quickly and deliberately. There was a never-resting orchestra of trains screeching on tracks, the high-pitched *meep-meeps* of tuk-tuks, announcements heralded every thirty seconds with a trumpet fanfare, and the dull roar of a thousand conversations.

Every few minutes, we were approached by someone who seemed to think that our clean clothes and white, nineteen-year-old faces presented an opportunity for them. Children offered cups of chai, older women brought platters of vegetable samosas. We denied all of their offers, not knowing yet if the tea was safe to drink or if the samosa was a deep-fried dysentery delight.

Then there were the beggars. Some were missing limbs, others had none at all. Faces and bodies destroyed by burns or ravaged by the most horrifying skin conditions. A steady parade of them had hobbled or dragged their way towards us relentlessly, their eyes pleading for money. They held out a hand or sometimes a stump, waiting for rupees. Indian travellers passing by looked at us and shrugged, shaking their heads. A university student apologised, telling us that we shouldn't hand over money, no matter how bad we felt, and that it was all a nasty scam. Somehow, this made us feel worse. We learned that if we looked at the beggars and shook our heads, it only seemed to make them stay longer, so we pretended to read our books and asked each other meaningless questions in pretend conversation in the hopes they would move on.

Twenty-four hours into the trip we'd certainly seen much of the extreme poverty I'd wondered about. If I were honest with myself, it was more overwhelming than I'd thought it would be. I was struggling to think how the graphs and theories I'd learned in economics class could apply in a place as chaotic and challenging as this. On the adventure front, we were well underway. Immediately out of the airport the night before, we'd walked into the thick New Delhi pollution and straight into the slick grasps of a conman. A rookie error. After three hours of trickery and a parade of shady characters, we'd decided to first *fight*, getting into a fistfight with the lead conman, and then *flight*, running into the smog and finally finding a place to sleep at three in the morning. Eager to leave the city that had made a bad first impression, we would now begin our loop around the country, heading east to Agra, home of the Taj Mahal.

When the Agra train pulled into Delhi, right on time, swarms of people surged towards it. We had very little money to sustain us for the next four weeks in India – less than $300 – so we had decided on third-class sleeper trains around the whole country, and the carriages we were seeing for the first time were colonially old and covered in a thick film of diesel, pollution and grime. At the steel stairs, the firm but friendly hands of other passengers grabbed us by our arms, shoulders and bag straps, and pulled us into a sweaty, squirming mass of travellers. I pulled my rucksack off and tried to sandwich it between my legs, balancing as best as possible as the train rocked and creaked its way south towards Agra. But I lost sight of it quickly as I was pushed farther into the crowd, a rookie failure my Lonely Planet guide had warned me about. I had my small backpack with me, which contained my passport and travellers' checks, but I was sure that my bigger bag of clothes was gone. But my frustration that I'd probably been fleeced was quickly replaced by discomfort, my left leg becoming numb as it was sandwiched against another traveller at an awkward angle. While it was cold outside, inside, the train quickly turned into a noisy, cramped furnace. I had no idea where Apples was, or whether he had even made it on board; I just hoped we would reunite in Agra.

Three hours in, my legs were sharp with pins and needles and my shirt soaked with sweat. I began to resign myself to another uncomfortable three hours before we reached Agra. The sun had set by now, and a dull, orange light cast shadows across the sea of faces, many of whom seemed to still be fascinated by me. Every seat was overloaded with three times more passengers than they were designed for. Some sat on the floor, and others squeezed their bodies awkwardly onto the baggage shelves over our heads. But then I felt a tap on my shoulder. It was Apples. Dressed in his tan North Face pants and a thin red Gore-Tex shirt, a wide grin on his face.

"I've got a seat, mate; follow me."

We pushed our way as politely as we could through the crowd, careful hands supporting us and smiles from all, friendly shakes of the head in the Indian manner from some. I sat down thankfully, bouncing my legs in an effort to bring circulation back to them, and then watched a small miracle unfold – my backpack being handed down the train compartment over the heads of the passengers.

"What do you make of this crew?" Apples asked as he pointed in front of him. This carriage was in stark contrast to the working-class men and women in the one I had just left. Here, a large group of much younger Indians were loudly singing, clapping and waving banners and flags around with great intent.

"Any idea what they are singing about?"

"Not sure."

They seemed excitable but harmless, but the group's singing increased in intensity as we rolled towards Agra, drowning out the clickety-clack rhythm of the train moving over the rails. With each stop, a few more squeezed into the carriage and joined them. Then an American flag was pulled out by one of them and tugged at aggressively by the group until it was torn to pieces. A printout of George W. Bush received the same treatment.

"Spud, are you watching this?" Apples murmured to me as he held his paperback up and pretended to read it.

I nodded. I saw what looked like the leader of the group: a tall, handsome guy in his twenties, his long hair pulled into a ponytail. He glared at us, his chin jutting out. I had seen this look plenty of times over the last few years in bars, usually when Apples had tried to flirt with someone's girlfriend. With a swoop of his right hand, the leader incited the others to sing louder, and they enthusiastically took up a new song. Then he made his way towards us, still singing, half a dozen friends in tow. Clearly, they were enjoying their strength in numbers.

He leaned over us, his eyes unblinking. "Do you know what it is we are singing about?"

We both shook our heads. Our lips were zipped.

"We are singing protest songs," he spat at us. "We are angry with what America is doing to this world. We are travelling to Kolkata for a rally. Are you Americans?"

"Nah," I replied quickly. "I'm from New Zealand, and he's from Tasmania, a tiny little place right down at the bottom of Australia." Apples leaned over to make a stronger case for his often-under-appreciated homeland, but he was interrupted.

"We are angry that America is fighting these wars in Afghanistan and Iraq. Do you agree with us, comrades?"

There was a focused look in his eye. Being called a comrade was a first for me – not a common term in the dull, nonpolitical suburbs I had grown up in. I didn't answer, because I could tell he had a whole speech lined up. If given a chance to respond, I might have had to admit that some of the actions taken by the US and its allies in Afghanistan I agreed with. September 11 had been such a horrendous act by Osama bin Laden and Al Qaeda. Maybe the Old Testament rule of an eye for an eye applied here. And from what I had read, the Taliban had ruled Afghanistan by absolute terror, particularly for women. So, if any war could be right, maybe this one was. But now was not the time to argue these points.

He told us his name, Mohammed, and with a short hesitation, remembering our briefings to not share our names too widely, I told him ours. He moved on to a new monologue, this one on the treatment of prisoners at Guantanamo Bay. I saw Apples flinch; he'd been struggling with this issue, researching it heavily and trying to figure out where he stood on the utilitarian ethics of torturing suspected terrorists during interrogations to protect the innocent. He'd started donating to Amnesty International.

Then Mohammed moved on to the subject of Iraq. I had been politely nodding through his tirades so far, but I stopped. I could hear myself swallowing, a sour taste each time. Iraq hadn't been invaded by land yet; it was still just the naval embargo. Indeed, the medals I had been awarded for my service the year before said Afghanistan on them because, officially, we weren't at war with Iraq yet. But he believed that a ground invasion was coming.

I had tried my best not to think about Iraq for the last year. But late at night, when I tried to sleep, the thoughts rolled in. I had dreams that I had actually died up there and never came home. That Crokes wasn't able to grab me. That I had been burned to death by that fireball. Or that I was no longer alive and only my parents were crying at my funeral. Sometimes, I thought about the smugglers we caught and, in particular, Farooq, the cook on *Fal 12*. Whether he was still alive. Of others trying to make a run through the embargo and being caught by the next boarding team that had been deployed to the Gulf. I'd shake these ideas out of my head, not willing to talk about them. I so desperately just wanted to be a young man who was not so serious, so burdened by what I had done so young in the Persian Gulf. To have a girlfriend, to enjoy a game of football, drink a beer without it leading to a fight. Mohammed kept going on and on, but Apples and I stayed silent. He moved onto the sanctions that had been placed on Iraq, which I had enforced, and I felt a heat rising in my chest. He'd done his homework, and I was shocked he knew about this mission. There were only a handful of boarding teams from the US, UK and Australian enforcing this.

He paused for a moment, out of angry opinions to hurl our way. We were the closest thing he had to a punching bag, and he wanted to take his rage out on someone. "You don't know about any of this, about all these people that are dying because of the West? You don't care."

The heat rose up in me and then foolishly came out. "I do know, mate. I enforced those sanctions on Iraq that you are talking about. We are both in the military."

Apples snapped his head my way. I didn't know whether I wanted to pick a fight with Mohammed or be his friend.

"You? Why did you do this? This thing you did will kill so many people!"

I wanted to tell him that I was too young to know any better. That it had all been part of this big adventure. That I wanted to be awarded medals because I thought they made us look tough. But I could only manage, "It was our job", as I shrugged my shoulders.

I saw his rage surge momentarily, but his shoulders dropped. He couldn't even look at me; maybe he couldn't believe that after all these protests and student rallies he had attended, he was meeting someone who had been a part of something he hated so much. "But how do you live with yourself, you have blood on your hands!" he sighed.

I didn't answer, but as I chewed on the inside of my cheek Mohammed told us what he had read about the sanctions. He believed that hundreds of thousands of people had died because of the mission, as food, medical supplies and basic necessities had slowed to a standstill. He told us he knew the sanctions were merely a precursor to a full-blown war against Iraq that would be coming soon. He couldn't believe we were still in the military after what we had seen.

We were all young. Passionate about the world and eager to make it better for those who were suffering. We moved closer to Agra, bouncing side to side with the rolling of the carriage across tracks laid by the blood and sweat of Indians, under the rule of the British, the homeland of all the men in my family. Apples seemed to enjoy the intellectual debate, still taking a stand on some points. But as I listened to Mohammed, I found I wasn't searching for counterarguments. In fact, if I was honest with myself, I was starting to agree with a lot of what he was saying.

Hours later, in the hostel we were staying at, I paid for an hour's internet access on the computer in the lobby. For the first time ever, I typed two words into Google: "Iraq Sanctions." I roughly knew that this mission had been started in response to Iraq's invasion of Kuwait in 1990. But as I read on, I learned the food rationing system introduced as a result brought the official calorie intake down to one thousand calories per day, less than half of that required for healthy living, and a policy that rapidly saw more than half of the population defined as living in extreme poverty.

I found a *60 Minutes* interview with Madeleine Albright, recorded in 1996 when she was the US Ambassador to the United Nations, in which she was asked, "Given that half a million Iraqi children have died – more than Hiroshima – do you think the price of these sanctions is worth it?" She replied, without hesitation, "We think the price is worth it."

Half a million children.

A tragedy worse than Hiroshima.

It was a tragedy in which I had played a role when the mission was at its most aggressive, softening up Iraq for the invasion to come.

Mohammed was right: I had blood on my hands. I looked down at them. They were shaking.

***

Four weeks and thousands of miles of railroad tracks later, we were in Northern Rajasthan. If our instructors at the Academy ever found out we had been this close to blacklisted Pakistan, we would be painting rocks as punishment for a year. We'd had the adventure we had sought and, determined to loop around the country in third-class trains, we had settled into a steady routine. Every few days we would move, arriving in new towns, eating at street-side food stalls, wrestling through stations to buy tickets, and watching the world go by from the open window of the trains we had called home. We had rarely opted to find a room for the night, instead finding ourselves sleeping in the streets, or back at the train station, excited to keep moving. The stubble on our young faces had grown into beards, and so too had our confidence as travellers. We had discarded the clothes that didn't seem right and picked up second-hand sandals, pants and shirts in roadside markets. The 1970s backpack I had taken from my parents had a bunch of new scuff marks and coughed up a cloud of dust if I gave it a slap. Our diet was made up of what we could buy with coins on the train from hawkers as they moved through the carriages with hot chai, sweet cakes, lukewarm samosas and watery vegetable curries. My stomach had held up okay, but Apples had exploded shit and vomit onto railway lines across the country. Poor bastard.

I'd tried to channel the painful discussions on the train to Agra, about the sanctions on Iraq and my role in them, into something more useful. In particular, I wondered if there was a way of righting my wrongs. Of bringing at least some balance back into the world. If I'd been part of something that harmed so many people, was there a way I could begin to help a different set of people?

I knew I could do little as a traveller living on $300 for the trip so I resolved to at least learn what I could. Many days, I found myself talking with the people who travelled in the same third-class carriages as us, mostly working-class, lower-caste Indians. They were curious about my life, and I was equally curious about theirs, so I listened for hours to their stories: about the realities of their lives, and the resilience they brought to each day. How they earned money. What they did when they got sick. The tragedies they had faced. The hopes they had for their children. I had a growing melancholy about going back to the military, and my heart sank when I pictured myself sitting in a lecture theatre in the coming semester, in my military uniform, my hair cut short, my face cleanly shaven, the cotton bracelets around my wrists cut off. I wanted so desperately to stay on the road and keep learning and keep exploring who I wanted to be. A man who could help to make the world better, rather than one who fought in wars that made it worse. One day, maybe, a humanitarian worker who could make a difference in places as difficult as those we had travelled through. Someone who didn't turn away from those who were suffering but turned towards them, ready to help. For now, this all felt so far out of reach. I still had years to serve on my military contract and this reality suffocated me.

It was our final week in India before we headed back to Australia for our second year at the Academy. We were moving from Jaisalmer to Jodhpur, this time by bus, and once again, due to overcrowding, we were sitting apart amid more than fifty passengers, a few dozen chickens and zero fans of deodorant. Bollywood music blared out, well beyond the ideal decibel level, from the tinny speakers, and flashing lights strung up around the bus pulsed with each dull bass beat.

I looked out the bus window to yet another township, past alleyways full of rubbish and row after row of tin-sheeted shanties. I thought about the first message I had sent to Apples on Instant Messenger that had instigated this trip:

Maybe one day we can use our degrees for something useful.

I just wished I could do that sooner. I yelled to him above the noise of the bus to get his attention. He turned and cupped his ear.

"Do you think there will ever be anything that we can do to help?" No-one noticed us. They were either asleep or consumed in their own conversations, shouting above the music. He shook his head. I guessed he wasn't impressed by my naivete.

"Big question, mate," he replied after a few seconds.

And he was right. But I had this hard-to-explain burst of optimism that I impatiently wanted to talk about right now.

"Any ideas?" he said.

"Ah, maybe. But … um … I'll get back to you." I sat down heavily as the driver changed gears with his two foot–long stick.

"You do that, mate," he said, and sat down, too. If I was the dreamer in our friendship, he was the realist, the one person who could bring me back to reality with a single sentence. He wasn't wrong. I knew it was audacious of me to think that I could apply basic principles of economics to a society as complex as India, or that a white outsider like me could have any answers to poverty.

That I could fix anything or even know what was broken. Where to start. That I didn't know what had been tried by all of the organisations, charities and government officials who had been working here for decades, centuries. But for every little voice telling me not to bother, that it was not my place to get involved, there was a louder one, somewhere deep in my soul, telling me that I should take part. Do something.

I yelled out to Apples again, and he turned around, taking off the headphones from his CD Walkman to listen. I could see a flash of annoyance this time. I asked him whether it would be possible to pay people a reasonable wage to pick up the trash on the streets. They could be paid by the bag, which they could take to a processing centre where others would sort through what they had collected, recycle what they could, and then dispose of what they couldn't. The streets would be cleaner. People would be healthier. Jobs would be created. There was money to be made.

He smacked it down quickly. "Pretty sure they are doing that already?"

I shrugged. I didn't know. He moved to put his headphones back in.

"I have another idea."

He kept the earbud close to his ear. I pointed out there were cows everywhere in India. Someone could make bottles, shopping bags and food containers out of a material that the cows would eat. When people were done with their packaging, they could throw it in the streets or in feeding bins. The cows would eat it. If no-one had to pay to feed their cows, they would have more money for their families.

"Are the holy cows allowed to eat rubbish?"

I shrugged again and sat down. Apples turned to face the front, but he kept one earbud in his hand. I knew him well enough to know that I had just tickled his brain.

"Pig shit?" he yelled a minute later, turning in his seat.

"Excuse me?" I replied, laughing. His idea was that pigs could be used to consume scrap food from restaurants, and the methane from their manure could be used for electricity production. We would have to work around the fact that many Muslims in India didn't like pigs, but it had merit.

It was the most exciting bus trip of my life. I wrote and wrote and wrote. For just a moment, I forgot about the life the military had planned out for me and stepped into one anew.

***

Later that week Apples and I returned to the Academy from India. When I stepped into my room I threw my trusty backpack on the ground, kicked off my dusty leather sandals, peeled off my filthy clothes that hadn't been washed in a week, reluctantly cut my two cotton bracelets off, shaved my hair short with a pair of clippers, and then sat down on the floor of the shower for an age, brown dirt trailing down the sink, and with it my freedom.

That first night I wrote in my journal.

Back. All I can think about is going again.

***

Sitting down six weeks later to work on yet another university essay, Apples yelled for me from the TV room. I headed down the hallway and into the lounge room, which was filled with thirty of my classmates, some in their sports tracksuits, some still in camouflage from weapons training, most with pizza boxes in their laps. Someone handed me a glass of beer, a 20-proof concoction that had been made in our latest hidden home brew setup. Everyone was watching the TV; George W. Bush was about to speak.

He was brief and looked straight into the camera, detailing the reasons why the "Coalition of the Willing" were invading

Iraq, a move in contradiction with the requests of the United Nations. "We are invading to disarm Iraq, to free its people, and to defend the world from grave danger," he said. He spoke of weapons of mass destruction, of bringing freedom to the people of Iraq, and that the US would accept "no outcome but victory".

I felt a lump building in my throat, my chest tightening with anger. I thought of the Iraqi people and the horror they would go through now. I thought of Farooq from *Fal 12* and his family. I thought of tanks, fighter jets and missiles hurling weapons into buildings. And of the body bags that would be sent home with people like us in them. We all watched quietly as history was made but when Bush was finished, I was the first to speak.

"This is wrong," I said across the room.

Half of my classmates turned around. I didn't think they knew what to believe. But I believed that a war wasn't needed in Iraq. This was an invasion.

A gung-ho, muscled rugby player, was quick to respond to me. "Oh fuck off, Spud; this is what we train for, man. This is sweet!"

The room laughed.

"Tell me one thing sweet about this," I said, pointing at the TV, my finger shaking. "People are going to die because of that speech. Iraqis. Americans, English, Aussies. Our mates are going to die because of this. Some of us might die."

I knew I was too loud. But before anyone could respond, a lanky officer wearing flannel pyjamas and woollen slippers, ran into the room, a six-pack of beers under one arm and an antique army helmet on his head. He had a toy gun in his hand – a small black pistol. "Yeeehaaa! We're going to war!" he screamed with delight.

Was I the only one who thought this was a tragedy? The only one who didn't want to go and fight? Sure, we needed to be warriors, and sometimes we needed to fight the right fights, but could we do that with compassion and some nobility? I tried to catch Apple's attention, but he was staring at the TV. I had to get out of there. Out of that room. Out of the military. Out of the wrong life I'd got myself into.

- TEN -

In my experience, most men take one of two options when they find themselves in turmoil.

They either find order in the chaos. They do good.

Or they choose bad, sometimes even descending into oblivion.

Like a metronome, I swung between these two extremes. On the side of order, I was obsessed with this vague notion of wanting to make a difference in the world and stayed up late each night reading about economics, politics and social justice. I dreamed of escaping the military and running off to some remote place – a refugee camp in central Africa, a slum or a favela in Brazil. If there were people in need, far away from my world, I wanted to escape there and begin to chip away at evening the ledger. To help more people than I'd harmed. Perhaps looking out for me, an Army captain invited me on a trip to hike the ten day–long Kokoda Trail in remote Papua New Guinea. We'd fundraised money and airdropped donations to clinics and gifts for the children along the way. In my backpack I'd tucked a book – *The Motorcycle Diaries* by Che Guevara. The travels through South America he wrote of in that book transformed him, and I began to wonder if the same kind of journey would change me, too. Maybe help me take some decisive action to leave the military and fully commit myself to a cause I saw as right and true.

But on the other extreme, my life was becoming crazier, and the nights of drinking and fighting more common. Sometimes, the metronome would swing to each side in the one night. I would go out drinking. I'd progressed from total shyness to now kissing girls, often several a night on the dance floor but only if I had enough Dutch courage with some drinks in me. But I didn't know how to take the next step. I'd usually flirt with the wrong girl and get in a fight with a stranger before being kicked out by the bouncers. I'd walk home by myself and fall asleep with a social justice book in my hand. The next morning would be a guaranteed hangover, and a shame-filled twenty-mile run to sweat it all out.

Guilt from my Christian childhood lingered, and I was irritated by the thought that my parents and my old friends were disappointed in me. Praying for my return to being a God-fearing, good boy. But I wanted so badly to be liberated. Politically. Philosophically. Sexually. I wasn't comfortable as Midshipman Aaron Tait anymore, the young military officer, and I wanted to shake free of this package deal of white, British, Christian values. Those were the ideals that I felt had got me into Iraq. I wanted to figure out who I could be if I broke free of the mould that had been set for me.

Armed with inspiration about South America from a social justice perspective and tempted by the lust and liberty I assumed of a place like Brazil, I booked an almost three month–long trip. To pay for it all, I'd broken a major rule at the Academy: working extra jobs. I'd searched in the newspaper, landing upon three days a week in the vineyards at a winery and in apple orchards over the weekends. It felt good to use my body for something as simple as providing food and wine for the world, rather than training it to be a better fighter. I had weaved an intricate web to cover my extra employment including paying off my classmates if any senior officers asked where I was. For the time I'd be in South America, my instructors at the Academy would think I was back at the diving branch continuing with my training towards being a Special Forces operative. At the same time the diving branch thought I was at the Academy continuing with my leadership studies. The military was so disorganised that it was easy to trick them into forgetting about me, which was brilliant because I wanted to forget about them as well. So much so that I didn't invite Apples along. On this trip I wouldn't be Spud. I wouldn't be a military officer. I wasn't checking my emails, and I didn't bring a phone with me. I was confident no-one would find out I'd escaped, but if they did, I barely cared about the consequences. Being kicked out of the military would have been fantastic at that point.

Like India, the plan was to loop around much of the continent, seeking out adventure, learning what I could. Starting in Chile, I would then move through the Andes into Argentina, north into the desert of Salar de Uyuni, up farther into the mountains of Bolivia, then along the Inca trails of Peru. Then I'd follow a line I'd drawn across the front-page map of my Lonely Planet guide, a horizontal route across the continent from Machu Picchu through the Amazon to the coast of Brazil for Carnival. It was there I thought I would find the oblivion I'd been seeking. Halcyon days where I could forget everything, and everyone.

Weeks into the trip I was in Potosí, a mining city in Southern Bolivia. I'd been invited for a tour into the silver mines where for a small fee I would be able to spend a day with the miners, to see how they lived and worked. At the opening to the cave, I'd seen the signs as I had walked in; the mine was owned by Australian, North American and British companies. The next plunderers in a long line of foreigners who had come to Bolivia for centuries to rip things out of this mountain. It was said the Spanish had taken enough out of Bolivia to pave a double-lane road to Madrid with silver. We descended deep into the mine, and I wondered for a moment how ethical it was that I was taking part in this tour. Whether perhaps I was even exploiting the horror of these men, just like the mining companies were.

But I pushed on, and for hours I explored this underworldly hell, where much of the work was done by hand. The short, hardened Bolivian miners bored holes into the stone with a chisel and a hammer before they rammed tubes of dynamite into them and ran for cover. Once the dust and rubble from each blast settled, the men shovelled the heavy stones into the carts and then transported them to the outside world. It was an ant mound of commerce, sliced into a maze of tunnels laid with rudimentary railway tracks. With little warning, carts laden with stones thundered down the slopes, death for anyone ahead who failed to dart out of the way in time. It was dark, and the only lighting was the torch on the helmets of miners and the occasional lantern or candle. The men, many of them half my size, worked at a furious pace, for twelve-hour shifts, six days a week.

"And in here is where we pray to Lucifer," my guide Rodrigo casually mentioned to me as we walked past a small room carved into the stone.

"As in Satan? The Devil?" I clarified, my hands on my knees as we leaned over in the small tunnel. The last time I had heard the word Lucifer was from the mouth of my youth pastor at a Pentecostal revival night. He'd been casting the demons out of his young flock, me included. Now, according to Rodrigo, I was in the devil's lair, and a very long way from youth group.

"*Si*, the devil," he said matter-of-factly, his bloodshot eyes glistening from the torch on his mining helmet. The devil's lair was deep in *Cerro Rico* – the Rich Mountain – two hundred metres underground but almost five thousand metres above sea level. The small amount of altitude we had lost as we had moved deeper into the mine on rickety mining carts had given only a small respite from the altitude sickness I was suffering.

"So why do you pray to Satan?" I asked as I wiped away a dribble of coca leaf from my chin, the raw material cocaine was made from. These leaves were the drug of choice down in the mine, ideal for the suppression of hunger and fear and increasing one's stamina. I had bought a plastic bag for me and one for Rodrigo.

"Because up there, in the world above, we pray to God. But down here, this is hell. And most of us will die before forty, so just in case we die down here, we pray to the devil."

He didn't stop for a moment to let what he had said sink in; it was delivered coldly. Just another part of the tour script. Stepping into the small room that served as both a shrine and a bar, Rodrigo pointed at the three-foot-tall wooden demon. Blood red, he sat on a throne, with a massive erect penis and enough booze and smokes to knock out even the roughest sailors I'd met.

Rodrigo nodded respectfully at the devil, then tapped me on the shoulder warmly. He was a short Bolivian man with leathery skin, callused hands and a warm smile. Barely thirty, he was a living testament to Oscar Wilde's description of a man's face being his autobiography. He already looked sixty, an age that, as I was just learning, he probably wouldn't make it to. But before I could let that sink in, the devil stole my attention.

I gazed right into Lucifer's eyes: his twisted red face, jet-black horns and sneering mouth packed full of cigarettes. At his feet were piles of coca leaves and small clear bottles of ethanol, the favourite drop of the miners. I sneered back at him.

The devil had been coming for me for a few years now. And recently, I knew that I'd been stumbling towards him. As a teenager I'd had it drilled into me that being good in the eyes of God meant simply not doing bad things. Don't drink. Don't masturbate. Don't swear. Good boy. But what had all that being good done for me, or for the world? I'd been the good boy and become the good officer in the fancy white uniform. That good officer had shipped off to fight in the good war. A war that was driven by oil. By some of the very mining companies that owned this hellhole of a mine I was down in.

As I sneered at Satan, good Aaron lost his grip. He convinced me to let hedonism win. That for the rest of my time in South America I shouldn't worry about being good. About doing good things in the world. No, I could lose myself in a blast of alcohol, drugs, and, hopefully soon, sex.

Rodrigo passed me a bottle of ethanol, terrifyingly close to 100 per cent alcohol. The strongest stuff I had ever tried was a 57 per cent ABV rum in the navy, and that had knocked me flat. He saw the moment of apprehension in my eyes. Satan peered at me over his shoulder. Rodrigo gave the bottle a friendly shake and nodded my way. "It's good for forgetting," he offered with a sad smile. I grabbed it quickly and took a swig. It was good for forgetting.

***

As I moved on from Bolivia and Peru and descended deeper into the Amazon, I let a feverish madness take hold of me. Life became a blur of cachaça shots in the rough bars of frontier towns, crossings of murky rivers, nights partying with gangsters, bags of coca and illegal border crossings. I snuck into Brazil without a visa, in a car with seven passengers, a dog, a giant turtle in my lap, a monkey next to me and a criminal fleeing the Peruvian police in the trunk.

I'd ended up in Caraíva, a village on the coast, in the centre of Brazil. It was a place that only had one paragraph of detail in my guidebook.

> *Only accessible by canoe, at the end of a 50-kilometre sandy road, Caraíva is a place for those who truly want to escape. No cars or infrastructure. Power is sporadic. Limited accommodation*

available in traditional wooden houses. Enquire with locals on arrival.

There I finally felt far enough away from reality. Like I'd truly escaped. My home was a small wooden hut on the beach, with a door that opened out onto the sand. I slept the best that I had in years and took long swims in the ocean. I spoke to no-one for days. I ate fresh fruit for breakfast and rice and vegetables at the same beach bar each afternoon. I took long siestas and lay under my mosquito net, naked in the heat. I wrote nothing in my journal, and my mind instead of being crowded and in turmoil was empty. At peace. I thought about very little. It felt incredible.

One afternoon I came out of the water and, wearing just my swimming shorts, headed up to the beach bar. It was a small wooden hut, painted in faded shades of orange and blue. I nodded at the owner, a young man with short black hair who I'd seen three days in a row, asking him in broken Portuguese for a plate and a cold beer and found a seat. He made his way out to the kitchen.

As I looked around, I saw a girl, about my age. She was lying down on a bed of cushions in the corner, her long, honey-brown legs stretched out. Her hair was dark brown, and she wore a bikini with a red, orange and pink pattern. Like a sunrise. A thin gold band was wrapped around one of her lean arms and I watched as she wrote some postcards. She glanced up at me and I quickly looked away; she was probably used to guys gazing at her like that. I faced the sea, watching as a storm worked itself into a rage. Lightning began to crack on the horizon. My drink came and, as the owner put it down, I took the opportunity to glance over at her again, but she definitely caught me this time and smiled, before looking away. A surge of embarrassment welled up in me, and I blushed. In a loud bar, with some alcohol-fuelled courage, I was better at all this, but sober, and with just the two of us there, the owner out the back, I was not as confident as I wished I could be. My food came and I finished it quickly, and as the storm crept closer to the coast, I stood up and paid.

Stepping onto the sand, I turned around for one final look at her. She was smiling at me. I smiled back and began to jog, ripe raindrops bursting onto the hot sand. I was dripping wet by the time I opened the door to my place, and I took off my shorts, pulled the mosquito net aside and lay down heavily on my bed.

As thunder rolled across Caraíva and flashes of light stole in between the cracks in the timber, lust rose through me like a fever. I fantasised about her opening the door, dripping wet from the rain. Walking slowly towards me and gently pulling apart the mosquito net, stepping inside it and kneeling over my body. Then unblinking, lowering slowly, filling herself with me. Without touching myself I came, and with my warmth across my stomach, I lay there, ashamed. Nervous I'd never see her again. Wishing I was more of a man and that I wasn't this pathetic virgin, alone once more. The fantasy continued to swirl through my mind late into the night, pushing any sleep away.

In the morning, I rose as the sun did and stepped out onto the beach. Still alone. The palm trees stood still, the wind yet to wake. The ocean was heavenly, with only the tiniest of waves breaking onto the white sand. I stepped through the shallows, diving in, holding my breath and pulling with long strokes through the water. Breaking back to the surface, I sat down in the shallows and looked up at the sky, a wild canvas of red, orange and pinks.

And then I saw her walking down the beach. Just ten yards from my shack. Wearing that same bikini. The gold band still wrapped around her arm. A pang of Christian shame raced up in me, but she couldn't possibly know about the lustful visions I'd had the night before. She stepped slowly into the water as I looked away, and I heard her dive under. Surfacing right by me, she pulled her hair back with her hands, looked straight at me and smiled again. I swallowed hard and smiled back.

"*Bom dia,*" she said, the first words we'd spoken.

"*Bom dia,*" I laughed.

"*Você fala português?*" she asked, a hint of shyness sneaking out from the boldness she'd just shown. *Shit, no I didn't.*

"*Um pouco, desculpe.* Do you speak English?" *God, I hope she did.*

"A little; sorry." She winced as her petite brown shoulders lifted up. She was even prettier up close. Her skin was goosepimpled from the water and her nipples pressed hard up against her bikini. A small wave pushed her close to me, her thigh rubbing against mine.

"Ah ..." She pointed at her chest. "São Paulo," she said. Then she pointed at me.

"Australia." I grinned and brought my hand to my chest. I felt my heart beating, and as I sat there she swam slowly in the shallows around me, our skin touching again momentarily.

She sat close to me, touched her chest again. "Viviane." And then she touched mine.

I think she felt my heart pounding because she giggled, but I got out an answer. "Aaron."

I could see her thinking about what to say, but without a shared language, she would hesitate and stay quiet. I did the same. How was this supposed to work? But we resigned to the silence, and she reached for my hand, running her index finger across it. Then she lay down in the water, between my legs, pulled herself up to look straight into my eyes and kissed me for a moment. But then she stood up quickly, walked out of the water and headed up the beach.

I breathed out a big sigh and shook my head. *Wow. What was that?* I laughed to myself, confused and delighted in the same breath. And not sure what to do with myself now, or if I'd ever see her again. Maybe that was enough. Or maybe she didn't even exist. Some fever dream, a siren sent by the devil in Bolivia.

I tried to go about my day. I thumbed through my travel guide, wondering how long I could stay in Caraíva before I needed to head to Rio and then, in a few weeks, catch my flight back to the Academy. The bus only went twice a week from here. I bought fresh passionfruit and pineapple, slicing it open at the front of my house with my hunting knife. I wondered what the boy Aaron would think of me now. Would he be proud? Or disappointed? I figured it was too early for him to make that judgement. I was still a work in progress.

Then, as I had each day, I went for a swim and headed up to my usual place. And there she was. Lying in the same spot as yesterday. Wearing that bikini, the gold band still around her arm. I sat down in my regular seat and smiled at her. This time, I held eye contact. So did she. A crack of lightning broke the sky, the storm more impatient today. The horizon was wild. With a moment of courage, I held out my hand and asked her to come with me. "*Vamos!*"

She stood up immediately and, laughing, we ran down the beach. Again, the rain burst onto the sand, hissing with each drop. I opened my door, and as we stepped inside, she fell into me, her tongue in my mouth. Mine in hers. The tin roof clattered as the sky opened and the timber walls shook as the wind drove in across the water. I took a step back to look at her, and as I did, she untied her bikini top which fell to the floor. She did the same with her bottoms, her pubic hair shaved close. Drops of water fell from her hair, and then from her dark nipples. She reached for my shorts, and as I stepped out of them and towards her, our lips were together again. I'd never been this close to a naked woman before, and I certainly never thought my first time would be with someone who looked like this. She reached for my hand and brought it to her breast, which rose and fell in my grasp. I grunted with primal pleasure, my breath quickening and my body rising. Then she brought my hand down to her wetness and I felt a warmth and a softness I'd never expected. An embarrassment rose up in me as I fumbled around, hoping I would find the right spot.

She pulled her face back from mine and looked at me.

"Ah … first for you?" she whispered.

"No," I lied and reached to try again. Then I leaned back and looked at her, my hands rubbing bashfully across my hips. "Ah … yes, actually. First for me." I could have died; and my face shot crimson, all my bravado vanishing in an instant.

She looked at me, smiled, and took both of my hands. She kissed my left eye. Then my right. She kissed my forehead. Both cheeks. My neck. My chest. And then my mouth. Deep and wet, both of us gasping for air. My body came back for me, and by my hand she led me over to the bed, pulling aside the mosquito net. I lay down on my back, and she sat just an inch above me, a knee on each side of my hips. I could feel her warmth. Then looking at me, blinking quickly, her wet hair dripping onto my chest, she slowly lowered herself onto me.

* * *

The late February sun slithered its way through the cheap curtains of my shack. My head was rested on one arm, and I gazed up at the ceiling. Viviane lay next to me, still asleep, her long hair splayed out on the pillow. A perfect breast snuck out from the thin sheet, and her naked leg was wrapped over me.

Using the Portuguese dictionary in the back of my Lonely Planet guide, we'd managed to communicate a few more things than our names and where we were from. She was an architecture student and had a boyfriend back in São Paulo, her first. He was a medical student, and they'd met at university. She was kind and loving. She had a mother and a father who were still together and a younger sister. She'd never done anything like this before. She was in Caraíva for only a few days to research the traditional homes here for an assignment. She needed to head back home soon. On our second day together, she had sat up naked in bed and, in broken English, said slowly, "Maybe tomorrow we never see our faces again, but this day we will enjoy each other." I kept finding a reason to stay one more day. So did she.

She learned that I was a student as well, studying literature and international relations. That I could be kind and loving too. That I had a mother and father who were still together and two brothers. That I'd never had a girlfriend before. That I needed to leave Caraíva soon as well. But there was a lot I didn't tell her. A lot that I didn't want to talk about. Perhaps she kept things from me too.

That morning, I carefully lifted Viviane's tanned leg off me and quietly got up from the bed. I sat down on the wooden chair and open my journal for the first time in a while to think about what was next for me. I knew what reality was, going back to the navy in a week's time. But I'd been on the run for this long, and I wondered how I could keep running, escaping, chasing this feeling of freedom. Of my youth. Of this pathway to this new person I was becoming.

I heard sheets rustling behind me and closed my journal without writing a word.

"*Bom dia,*" Viviane said sleepily from the bed. I looked around, and she was sitting up, twirling her arms to the sky, seductive shadows dancing on the wall behind her. Then she reached out her arms to me.

I could start figuring my life out tomorrow.

- ELEVEN -

Coming back from Brazil to the Academy was harder than ever. No-one was the wiser that I'd been away, and when I was back, to me it felt like very little about the place had changed. Most of my classmates were still heading out to the same bars each weekend, drinking the same drinks and having the same old conversations.

But I felt a big change in myself. I'd fallen in love with the freedom I'd had in South America and I was desperate for more of it. And if my time with Viviane had taught me anything, it was that if I wanted something, I had to be bold enough to make it clear to the world. My first day back in Australia I'd written down a line from Thoreau on a piece of paper and stuck it to the wall right next to my computer so I would see it throughout the day.

> *"I went to the woods because I wished to live deliberately… and not, when I came to die, discover that I had not lived. I wanted to live deep and suck out all the marrow of life."*

My next escape came much easier than I thought it would. I realised that in the eyes of the navy, our three years at the Academy had only two goals. First, that we completed our military leadership training. I'd already done this; indeed, Apples and

I had traded places in the winning of awards across the last two years, which baffled both of us. The second was to graduate with our academic degrees. I'd taken double loads the year before, curious about a range of subjects and had passed them all. If I took one more semester of double courses, I'd be done by July. By my logic I'd be fine to take leave without pay for July to January and meet up with my classmates in the new year, saving the government money.

Convinced that this was a win-win, I precociously booked flights to Spain. And my reasons were not noble. After Viviane returned to São Paulo I was emboldened with a newfound feeling of daring and brashness. On the way south and then in Rio de Janeiro for Carnival I had thoroughly enjoyed myself. The Brazilian spirit made things much easier, and life was a blur of forró dancefloors and lust-filled beds. It seemed every beautiful woman I was with was up for a good time without obligations. Sometimes several were.

I'd gone long stretches forgetting I was in the military. Forgetting the guilt I'd built up on my shoulders. I'd almost forgotten the desire I'd had to do good in the world.

But the moment I arrived back at the Academy, and someone called me Spud, it all came rushing back. That tightness in my head and chest. The feeling I couldn't escape, like a wild animal with its leg in a trap.

When I asked for a meeting with my senior officer, a desk-bound bureaucrat who had failed specialty training, she laughed in my face. With her hair pulled so tight into a bun that it looked like her cheeks had been pulled up too, she chuckled to herself while she shook her head. "Aaron, I can guarantee that is not going to happen."

I smiled politely, picked up my leave application from the desk and left the meeting. I was so sure of myself that my pulse didn't increase by a beat. I walked down, without an appointment, to the base psychologist for the first time ever. I told the receptionist politely that I was happy to wait in the lobby for an opening. The psychologist, a tall, fit woman who ran marathons as a hobby, welcomed me five minutes later with open arms; by the time I was buying her lunch, she'd diagnosed me with post-traumatic stress and signed off on the rest of the year as leave without pay. The psychologist had deployed with army units to both Afghanistan and Iraq, and her putting a diagnosable name on what had been going through my brain felt important. Suddenly, the alcohol I'd been drinking, the fights I'd been getting into in bars, the numbness I'd felt and the desire to put myself into life-or-death situations while travelling all made sense. It was powerful to know that I had something wrong with me, and that it could be fixed. And the fix was to get away, again.

***

"*Una caña, por favor.*" I nodded confidently at the tanned barman, knowing full well that my Spanish would run out quickly if he chose to engage in any real conversation. He had smirked and moved to the beer tap, a Manchester United game playing on the TV behind him. "Haha, you speak Spanish like a Chinaman! *UNA CANA OF CERVEZA* for the Chinaman coming right up," he teased in an English accent and placed an ice-cold glass of Estrella in front of me, effervescent froth spilling onto the wooden bar. "This one's on me, mate," he said, and winked. *Excellent.*

I was still pinching myself that my plan had worked, and that I was now in Alicante, an old town on the coast, south of Valencia. And my beer was already empty.

"*Un otra,*" the barman said. He had apparently decided for me and began pouring. "Want a job too?"

I had put my CV up on an online jobs board, hoping to make use of my naval training and find some work on the superyachts, but the only response I had received was from an escort agency. They had asked for some photos, which I had provided, and they had then replied the same day with a job offer. They would pay for my travel to Malaga to start next week. The role was to be a male escort for wealthy women across the Mediterranean. I could determine what I was willing to do sexually, and the jobs could be as short as a night, and as long as a week. I would be paid a set fee for each engagement, plus tips, and when I was with a client, they would cover all expenses. A flattering option, but probably a last resort.

"A job, yeah, I'm interested. I was planning on heading to the marina tomorrow to see if I can find something on one of the boats, but …"

He gave me directions to a nightclub up the road and told me to ask for Alex who I spotted fifteen minutes later as I walked in through the doors. He was seated at the back, in stonewashed jeans that were so torn that they showed off his bleached Calvin Kleins, leather boots with no socks and a crisp white singlet that accentuated his deep tan. Under each arm sat a gorgeous girl. When I told him that Jimmy had sent me about a job, he took me up to the bar and gave me the rundown. €1,000 a month and I could stay with him if I needed a place. But then he said that I had to pass the interview first, which was to steal one his girls off him and take her home that night. I started work the next day. If I thought Brazil was fun, this was a whole new league. Life became one big blurry, never-ending party. We had VIP status with every club owner and drug dealer in town, and after our club closed, we went straight to the front of every line and made full use of everything at our disposal. Weeks blended into one, with a succession of one-night stands, and the house that Alex and I shared became known as the United Nations. So named not for any noble causes we were forwarding, but because of diverse nationalities of women who shared our beds. All the girls seemed happy with the situation. One night of partying and fun was the only guarantee; the summer was too short to promise anything else.

The club was our playground, and we drank, smoked and took all the free drugs we wanted. Everything was in cash, and with very little bookkeeping happening, I often took the liberty to give myself a little bonus straight from the till when I was short on euros. If it was too hot inside for clothes, most of them were removed. I kissed five new girls every night and went home with my favourites. I pierced my ears and grew my hair long. It was all so much fun, until it wasn't.

***

One Monday afternoon, after another weekend of debauchery in the club, I lay naked, stretched out on my bed, fighting off delirium from the suffocating afternoon heat I had woken up in. All the sheets kicked off. A broken fan spun slowly next to me, the only item I owned other than a small backpack of clothes. I heard the door click shut downstairs as the girl from the night before left. She was French, and I didn't know her name. I didn't know what we had talked about or what I had said that brought her to my bed; and it was nothing against her, but I didn't want to see her again. I stared vacantly at the ceiling, paint peeling from the hundred-year-old stucco. My foot dangled to the floor, cold on the mosaic tiles.

I was so fucking bored.

Which was really annoying.

On almost every count, I should have been ecstatic, enjoying each night what many young men all over the world would dream of. I didn't know if it was a cocktail of everything I had been drinking, sniffing and smoking, or if depression was coming for me, but literally nothing moved through my mind, and I just stared up at that damn ceiling. I hadn't spoken to anyone who actually cared about me for way too long. No emails, calls or letters home. My friends and family didn't know where I was or if I was even alive. I would later find out that my parents had started calling embassies, asking if my body had been found anywhere.

Out in the lounge, the TV was on, and mindless commentary from the Athens Olympics competed with the sound of the street below. I felt like a bird had done a shit in my mouth and I'd been hit in the head with a baseball bat. It was clear that I'd drunk way too much again last night. I was so thirsty and, after a time, I reached down to feel for a glass of water on the floor, but my hand rested instead on my journal. I leaned back, flicked through it, and closed one eye to minimise the headache; I read of a moment when I had been in the highlands of Papua New Guinea, lying flat like this, but sober and happy while the village choir sang as the sun went down. I had felt so good there, useful, even if we'd only brought in a few boxes of donations. On another page was an entry from the bus in India when Apples and I had been coming up with ideas to make things better. I liked the Aaron on these pages.

I wondered what life would be like if I woke up as this Aaron every day. I kept flicking through the pages and came across a quote from JFK I had scribbled down. Happiness, he'd said, was "*the full use of one's powers along lines of excellence*". I blew out deeply, my lips trumpeting, then slapped the journal shut and let it rest up against my bare, sweating chest, chemicals from the night before slowly working their way out. I was so far from that. Running off and being a humanitarian worker was not possible. I was a twenty-year-old who had to go back to the military – I still owed them another three years. But I so wanted to live deliberately, to become the "good" me so much sooner. The metronome felt like it wanted to swing back to the good side, where I'd made a positive difference, but it had been stuck hard to the other side for a while now, as I'd indulged in debauchery, and in myself.

I felt like I needed to go somewhere quiet and get away from Sin City – Alicante. I headed to the cybercafé and found a cheap flight to Scotland for later in the year. I figured I'd still enjoy the summer.

And then I headed to the ocean, determined to swim across Playa del Postiguet. A baptism of sorts, and a fresh beginning. I resolved to do it every day until I left Alicante.

***

On September 11, exactly four years since I'd deployed to the Middle East, I walked barefoot down to the beach, wearing only my shorts. It was crowded, with thousands of people dotted along the white sand and swimming in the turquoise waters. I made my way across the boulders of the break wall until all the people were little spots; the only noise that far away were the waves crashing on the rocks. The swell was big, and I was a thousand feet from the sand. The breeze was strong out here too. It felt good.

The waves surged in and out and I waited for a moment, then dove in, the water salty on my eyes, and colder than it was in closer. I looked over my shoulder at the break wall, but it was too rough to turn back now, and the current was already pulling me away. So I put my head down and looked down into the familiar but haunting abyss of the deep ocean below me. I began to freestyle across the dark, open water and moved through the initial stage of fatigue and shortness of breath to settle into a rhythm: four strokes, two kicks and a breath; four strokes, two kicks and a breath. I closed my eyes in the water but opened them as I rolled my head to the sky, blue and wide.

An hour or so in, I turned over and lay on my back to rest. The Mediterranean water was warm and salty and held me up with buoyant care. I breathed in and out deeply, my body sinking slightly with each exhale and the water enclosing around my face, and then floating up with each big inhale. Small waves slapped against my head, the sound muffled with my ears underwater. The sun danced on my eyelids, and transparent rings shot like little tadpoles across the pink, moving from the centre before disappearing away. I played with them, seeing if I could hold them for just a few seconds longer. But then each of them seemed to bring a memory with them. Memories that I usually buried as quickly as I could. Of Iraq. Of Trent's death. But this time, now that I had learned to keep the darting rings in my eyelids for just a moment longer, I let the memories stay with me. I floated for a long time, and memories flashed in and then slowly slid away when they were ready. Then, from somewhere deep inside, I felt a heat up my spine, up into my heart, along my shoulders to my fingertips, and then up my neck and into my head. I wasn't fighting it, and it swirled around my body, spinning faster and faster, and then, finally, the tears came.

Big guttural sobs pulsed through me, and the salt from my eyes married with the Mediterranean. I cried and cried and cried. I felt so lonely, like there was no-one on the planet whom I could talk to who would truly listen and understand. Certainly not in this crazy town.

When the tears were all cried out, I turned over and freestyled the last mile. I felt the sand up against my feet. I stepped out of the water and walked back along the beach, mentally and physically shot. The afternoon sun was low in the sky. Heading for home, I spotted Alex, who got up from his towel and ran towards me. I recognised the girl next to him, a Russian stripper he had been dating over the weekend.

"Where have you been, man? This Russian chick's friend likes you; we all gonna have some fun tonight. You can pick the one you like." He had wrapped his arm around my shoulder. "Also, there is a big group of Americans just up there. They look new.

Use that Australian accent of yours and do what you do." I told him I wasn't feeling it, but that if he did the talking, I would come with him. I just wanted to go home for a shower and some dinner before the club opened.

As we neared them, my motivation dropped even further. They looked like every new intake of American students spending their semester abroad – huge groups, often thirty or more, stretched out on the sand, hip-hop music playing. I was already looking past them, thinking how to tell Alex that I was going to split.

But then one of the Americans caught my attention. She was gorgeous, lying face down, her sun-bleached blonde hair hanging messily over her shoulders. There were plenty of pretty girls in this town, but she felt instantly different, and I couldn't understand why. It was like everyone, and their towels and umbrellas, had been lifted off the beach like wired-up actors off a stage, and suddenly she was the only one left. But I had zero effect on her; in fact, she hadn't even looked up. She was engrossed in her book, an orange Penguin paperback. She was also the only person in the group not listening to Alex talk about how great our club was.

I'll be the first to admit that I'd swung from love interest to love interest at a rapid pace that year, still in shock that I'd figured out how to actually make things happen with women. But I'd also slowed down since the French girl. The party had become old.

But this girl. *Who is she?* My mood swung on a dime. I had to get these Americans into our club, and I had to talk with her. There were thousands of students on the beach every day, and enough rival clubs in Alicante to mean that if we didn't get them through our doors that night, I might never see her again. Alex was doing well with them, but I decided to up the stakes.

"Okay, team," I said as I rubbed my hands together. "The clubs all open later tonight, but let's say we all go right now, just us, and we get the party started early. Drinks are on me." They weren't really on me; they were on the boss, but he wouldn't find out.

The Americans were all in. Of course they were. Nothing says good times like "drinks are on me" to poor students. They shook the sand off their towels and packed away their American footballs and Frisbees into their backpacks.

I walked up the beach, and then up the main street of town, thirty American students following me. I opened the club, asked the last person to close the door behind us when we were all inside, pressed play on the music, and started serving up shots of tequila. But I couldn't see her. Surely, she was in here somewhere. I served up another round of shots to a group of guys in Hawaiian polo shirts and then leaned across to one of them, his NBA hat on backwards. "Hey, there was a blonde girl in your group," I said.

He nodded and pursed his lips. "Smokin' hot? Red bikini? Amazing tits and ass?"

"Yeah," I replied quickly, feeling like she was something more special than that characterisation. "I don't think she came with you guys; she was reading a book."

"Dude, impossible," another guy nodded, his front teeth biting his bottom lip "We all been tryin', that's for sure. Even the girls!"

"But is she here, though?" I asked.

"No, man, different league that one. Plenty of other fish in the sea!"

I had just blown a few hundred euros of the boss's money on drinks, and she hadn't come in.

For the rest of the night, I couldn't stop thinking about her. Her face. Pretty, bright, warm. That blonde hair tucked behind her ears with piercings all the way up each side. Her tanned legs stretched out on her towel, crossed at the feet. Little colourful bracelets on each ankle. How she had never looked up from her book. I went through the motions, kissing friends on the cheek as they came in, pouring drinks and ringing the bell each time we got a tip. At around midnight, when I didn't seem jovial enough for the boss, he sat me down, and we did Jack Daniels shots until he was convinced I had cheered up. His long brown hair bounced as he danced his way back to his group of girls. That night, for the first time in a while, I left the club and walked home by myself.

For a few afternoons, I walked the beach but didn't see her. I even bumped into some of the American guys, but they weren't helpful and just asked me when the next free drinks were on. So, I decided to organise the biggest party of the summer. I spent the week putting up posters on as many walls and bus stops as I could, with an offer too good for any person under twenty-five with a pulse to refuse: 3 for 1. I would just tell the staff to fill the glasses with ice and do four-second pours instead of six, but still, everyone would think it was the deal of the year. I called in every favour I could to promote the night and told everyone to come, bring all of their friends and spread the word. My thinking was that if half the town showed up, surely she would stroll in, too.

Now, on Wednesday night, there was a line down the street. People were trying so hard to get in that Patrick, our massive doorman and a bare-knuckle boxer from Northern England, had already made mincemeat of someone in the street and was on the run from the police, the rumour spreading among the staff that one of the boss's men was driving him to Portugal. By midnight, we had moved more money through the tills than any night of the summer.

But most importantly, at about 10pm, she walked in. Effortlessly stunning. No makeup. Alex saw her too and yelled to me, "Water and soap," an Italian turn of phrase for the kind of girl who needed nothing but water and soap to look beautiful. Her hair in a rough ponytail now. Silver bracelets shining bright on her tanned wrists. A white singlet, with thin white straps. Stonewashed Levi's. Simple black sandals.

I gave her ten minutes to settle in, and then, in between serving the crowd, I seized the moment. I leaned over the bar and touched her lightly on the arm to get her attention over the music. She leaned over, her face close to mine; smiling, I said only three words: "You are incredible," and then I leaned back and served the next customer.

As I made their drinks, three each, I glanced up at her and grinned. So did she.

At midnight, the club was as full as I had ever seen it, and the party was in full swing. The staff gave up and were just enjoying themselves, making out with their picks for the night and pouring whatever we had left on the shelves for free. Javier, the DJ, blew a kiss from the DJ booth and mixed in "No Rain" by Blind Melon, a song he knew I loved, and a fresh respite from the house music he had been pumping all night. I saluted with two fingers to him, and he gave me a proper military salute back. It was time for me to take a break and to find her.

I stepped up on the bar and jumped down into the crowd, dancing my way through. I walked up to her group as she danced, smiled, and stretched out my hand to her. Her face lit up, and she reached out hers to me, petite, elegant and warm, interlocking her fingers through mine, an immediate intimacy that made my heart race. I felt the simple rings she wore on each finger and led as we wove through the crowd, past the bar and into the back storeroom, where wine was piled high and a dim bulb that barely lit our faces swayed on its cord. I leaned back against boxes of Rioja. She leaned in, brought her hands up to the side of my face, and we kissed, and kissed and kissed. I felt tears that wanted to escape my eyes, but not wanting her to see, I kept my face close to hers. As one of us would lean back, the other leant in, desperate for more. Desperate for each other. Like we'd been floating through life, but now our souls had touched, and they didn't want to let go.

Finally, I wrapped my arms around her waist and leaned my head back and looked at her, her hands still on my cheeks.

"Hi," I smiled. "I'm Aaron."

"Nice to meet you, Aaron," she laughed, leaning her head to the side. "I'm Kaitlin."

"Nice to meet you, too, Kaitlin," I chuckled. "Do you want to get out of here?"

"Sure," she said, biting her bottom lip.

Our fingers interlocked again, and we snuck out through the crowd and into the street. We walked side by side through people smoking, chatting and laughing on the sidewalks, the pulsing bass of the club fading into the distance and past the rival clubs, all empty. Past the hashish dealers, who gave me a wave. Down La Rambla and into a wine bar my friend ran in the old town. We hid in the corner and sipped on Malbec. We talked and talked and talked, sometimes kissed. She was studying Psychology and Spanish. She would be in Alicante until the end of the year. She had just broken up with her boyfriend back at her private university in California. She was immersed in *Love in the Time of Cholera* by Márquez. She had been reading Pablo Neruda to practise her Spanish. Next weekend she was heading to Granada to see the Alhambra, and she couldn't wait. She liked to listen to Joni Mitchell, Bob Dylan and Fleetwood Mac. She had spent her last summer volunteering in Mexico with Habitat for Humanity. I answered some of her questions but held back a lot and when she asked why I was in Spain, I gave my regular line – I was escaping something.

Our Malbecs finished, we left the wine bar, hand in hand. The morning light shone on the old fort that looked over Alicante, and we walked to her home. I kissed her good morning on the steps of her place.

"I'd really like to see you again?" I whispered as she put the key into her door, careful not to wake the Spanish family she was living with.

"I'd love that," she whispered back.

We stole one more kiss, let our hands go, and I heard her walking up her stairs. It wasn't lust I felt. I just wanted her to come back down and put her hand in mine again. I wanted to swim in the ocean with her. To kiss her again. Learn more about her. But I heard a door click shut and knew I'd have to wait.

The city was beginning to wake up now; the street cleaners sprayed the pavement, bottles clattered into bins, residents cycled to their jobs. Too excited to sleep, I headed to my favourite morning place, a workman joint that served breakfast to tradesmen starting their days. No-one in there spoke a word of English, but familiar faces greeted me in Spanish as I entered. I pulled up a seat at the bar, the previous night's Barcelona game playing on the old TV in the corner. "*Buenos días, señor, bienvenido,*" the owner said, dipping his head to me as he wiped down the stone counter with an old cloth, his thinning black hair slicked flat over his balding scalp and his belly bulging over his grimy waist apron.

"*Buenos días, señor, gracias,*" I said, making sure to pronounce my *c* as a *th* sound in the Spanish way.

He already knew my order, a *bocadillo* filled with tortilla and jamon, which he placed down in front of me. Thirty seconds later, after some well-rehearsed clanks and clinks from the coffee machine, a double shot of espresso with a slight dash of whiskey.

"*Cómo estás?*" he asked as he laid a paper napkin next to my cup.

"*Muy bien, señor,*" I grinned. "*De hecho, estoy enamorado.*"

A wide smile creased his face, the wrinkles bunching up around his eyes. He reached across the bar and grabbed both of my hands with his. The old men around me nodded warmly and tutted their approval.

I was very good, I had told him.

In fact, I was in love. For the first time in my life.

* * *

The coffee cups were warm in my hands as I walked quietly down the hallway of my old Spanish apartment, stucco falling off the ancient walls, my feet cold on the stone floors. Van Morrison played quietly; *Astral Weeks*.

I had woken as Alicante did, the sounds of children walking to school, friends greeting each other in the street, bicycles ringing their bells. I had woken rested. Happy. I had woken in a bed I had shared with Kaitlin for most nights of the last six blissful weeks. Dressed in my disintegrating jeans I had worn most days since I had bought them in Argentina, I stepped into the front room – faded red linen curtains blew in the breeze, cooler now that November was nearing.

There she was. A picture. Sitting in her underwear on a wooden chair on the balcony that looked over the street, her brown legs popped up on one another. She wrote in her journal. I paused to take in the scene. It was one I would maybe never see again.

On our first real date I'd met her at Mercado Central, and as I'd walked up to her, she was speaking with an old fruit-seller in fluent Spanish. He was so charmed he'd given her a free peach and a kiss on each cheek. When she asked me what I was escaping from, I told her everything. That I was in the military. I told her how it had all started like a big adventure. That I'd come home with medals and war stories. But that I began to realise I had played a part in a military operation that had been a humanitarian catastrophe, made worse by the war now being fought. I told her how terrible I felt about it all and that I needed to right my wrongs somehow. Perhaps by doing a whole lot of good in the world to bring some balance back. I spoke about how for the last few years I'd been escaping, that it wasn't just a throwaway line. Escaping through drinking, girls and disappearing from those who love me most. How my parents, brothers and my best friends had no idea where I was and hadn't since I left Australia.

She'd told me about her reality. San Francisco. A few more

years of college. But that she wanted to get out of the U.S for a bit and that she had dreams of packing up and helping somewhere. South America maybe, or somewhere in Africa.

The last six weeks had been the happiest of my life.

We had woken each morning wrapped up in each other. We made coffee, dressed, then walked into our day, lifting our hands over the three-foot-high pole just before we turned left and into the bakery for *ensaïmadas*. She went to class, and I headed to the beach to run and exercise, swim the bay, read and write. In the afternoon, we took siesta and then lay in bed and talked through whatever lessons she'd had that day: philosophy, literature, politics. Dinner was often a seafood paella for two and a carafe of wine at the outside table of a quiet restaurant before I raced my way through a shift at the club while she hung out in wine bars with our Spanish friends. Then we met up, danced, laughed and drank cheap Rioja. We walked home hand in hand through cobblestone streets, stopping to kiss under old streetlights, and then made love and fell asleep in each other's arms, ready to do it all again the next day.

We talked for hours about living a big life, travelling the world and making a difference. We dreamed of the ways we'd like to be of use in the world: she wanted to work with women and children; I had started to feel like I wanted to try to come up with useful economic solutions. But we were both guarded – we didn't speak of our futures as one. It was a defence mechanism; we knew that this salty, golden-hued summer would soon come to an end. We were twenty-one years old. We had no money. She would soon return to California to finish two more years of college, and I would return to the navy to serve out the final years of my contract. The thought was devastating to consider, but these six beautiful weeks might have been all we would ever have, and each perfectly simple day we shared took us closer to the last one that we would be together.

I parted the curtains carefully with a coffee mug in each hand, leaned over and we kissed – long, warm and maybe enough to encourage her to come back to bed. But she motioned to the opposite chair, and when I sat, she tucked her ankles in alongside my hips. I knew not to ask her what she was writing about; our journals were the one place just for ourselves. She put her pen down.

"I'm writing about you," she said, smiling, "and me, and us, and all this." And she put her hand on her chest.

I looked out across the street from our second-floor balcony and smiled. "Best summer of my life."

"Mine too." She kissed me again.

***

But even the best summers must end.

The date of my flight to Scotland, once far on the horizon, came around too quickly. There was no benefit in changing it. Kaitlin's final weeks in Spain would see her travelling to towns and cities across the country to finish her university semester. We agreed to meet at the castle for sunset. One last moment together before I caught a lift to the airport.

I packed up my things, left my bag at the club and then made my way to the base of Castillo de Santa Bárbara, the ninth-century fort that looked over Alicante. I arrived early and sat down on the first row of stone stairs.

We both knew that this was probably it for us. She would return to America, maybe meet a responsible guy, get a job in the city, take out a mortgage and have some kids. I would meet someone, too, and have my own life. Tomorrow I would be hundreds of miles away; soon it would be eight thousand. A devastatingly long distance. This was the first time I had ever been in love, which meant it was the first time I would have my heart broken.

When I saw her come around the corner and walk up the stone stairs at the base of the castle, I felt dread move through me. How could I bring myself to say goodbye to her tonight? She was prettier than ever. Her hair golden from the summer, her skin a fine caramel and, as usual, no makeup. Over her shoulder, she wore a small brown leather bag, with a Walkman, a book and an envelope sticking out of it. We kissed, wove our hands together and started up the castle.

We slipped into a familiar rhythm, like we had known each other for years, not the six weeks we'd had together. She talked about her day, we laughed about funny characters we had met over the summer, and she told me about a trip she had planned to Madrid. At the top of the castle, we sat on a bench, the sunset lighting up the blond stone walls of the city. The Mediterranean on one side, the mountains on the other. The town was laid out below us. The beach where I'd first seen her. The bar where we'd kissed. The Plaza de Torros bullring by her house. We didn't say much for a while. Just held hands and looked out over the horizon. The thought that we soon wouldn't be able to hold each other felt hard to comprehend.

I tried to lighten the mood. "Maybe when we're forty, I'll walk into a bar in New York or London and, by some miracle, you'll be in there, too. We'll bump into each other. You'll be drinking a margarita, I'll order a whiskey. And then we'll catch up on how our lives played out and laugh about this one amazing summer twenty years earlier. You'll show me photos of your kids, and I'll show you mine." When I said that, my voice caught, but I tried to be funny. "You'll tell me about your husband, and I won't like him. You won't like my wife either." She smiled at me and squeezed my hand, and we went quiet again.

We walked slowly down the castle. She wanted to walk home alone, and I needed to message Alex and head to the airport.

So, this was it.

Time to say goodbye, in this empty side street in the old town.

We hugged for a long time. Kissed for longer still. I held her hands and stepped back to take one last look at her, to try to capture every last bit. A black leather necklace with a golden amulet. Her many rings across her fingers. Faded pink jeans, a white peasant blouse, the front strings hanging open and loose. Her face perfect, her golden hair with a strand hanging over her eyes, tears in them, and in mine.

I reached into my pocket and handed her a letter, written in small blue ink on the inside page of my copy of *The Metaphysical Poets*. She put it in her back pocket and handed me an envelope, with "aaron" written on the front in lowercase.

We kissed one more time, neither of us wanting to let go, our tears bitter in our mouths, and then she pushed me away.

"Go."

I took the momentum she had gifted to me. Ten paces later, I glanced around over my shoulder, but she wasn't looking. She was walking down the street, in the other direction. Maybe the love of my life, now out of my life.

- TWELVE -

SCOTLAND WAS EVERYTHING I'd hoped it would be. Cold. Rugged. Wild.

With a broken heart I hitchhiked from Glasgow up to the Isle of Skye and then back down to Edinburgh. I spent melancholic days hiking up Munros, Scotland's green, bald, windswept mountains. On these walks, I was often completely alone and, with so much time, worked my way through my thoughts. I didn't drink and had no desire to meet any women. Memories of Iraq came into my head, and I saw them come and then saw them go, blowing away and into the valley. Forever taken by the Scottish haar. The desperation I'd so often felt about returning to the military was fading, replaced with a stoicism to get my time done. I even thought about Trent for the first time in years. His family was Scottish, too, and I knew he would have loved it up here. But when he came into my mind, the sadness I'd refused to deal with was gone, I just felt joy about all the smiles I'd always seen him bring into every room he entered in the short time I knew him. I realised that my response to his death had been selfish; this desire to live this big, full life, to be remembered, was humbled up in those mountains. Replaced by a simpler feeling that I just simply wanted to live my life with grace and acceptance. That if I was good, that was enough.

I resolved that in Edinburgh I'd climb Arthur's Seat, a little smaller than a Munro, so classified as a Marilyn instead. I smiled when I'd read that at the start of the walk and then headed for the summit, an easy stroll. I felt light. Free.

Near the top I took a moment to catch my breath and looked twenty yards up. A fine sleet curled around the ragged slabs of rock, and a fine wind whistled through the valley. My hair, which I hadn't cut for almost a year, blew in my face. I would soon need to find a barber and get it buzzed close before I returned to the military.

I was the only one up there. I sat down on a tussock of grass among the stone, opened my backpack and pulled out my lunch: Tesco sausages I'd cooked earlier that morning in the hostel, two crusty rolls, two squares of dark chocolate and a bottle of cider. I pulled out my hunting knife, its weight familiar and trusted in my hand. I sliced the sausages, placed them in the rolls, which I put down on a stone, and then cleaned the knife on long grass. My hands cold, I ran my index finger along the engravings. *Far Horizons.* The initials of my grandfather, *PK*, and my father, *Iain*.

I opened my journal; inside the cover, there was a small picture of Kaitlin looking straight into the camera, my only photo of her. "Far Horizons" was written in big letters across the top. I'd come to fully embrace it in Scotland and realised that up to then I'd never entirely allowed myself to be my father's son. I'd felt for years like I needed to run away from him, from Christianity, and from that military legacy the Tait men had been tied to. With humility I was starting to admit we were more alike than I'd first believed. He'd left the military for love and adventure. He was a man of purpose and passion. One day I'd have to tell him I loved him. My mother too.

I twisted off the lid of the cider, took a bite of a roll and started to write, looking up every now and then over Edinburgh.

You could see much of the city from up there: Edinburgh Castle, the Water of Leith, the Royal Mile, Holyroodhouse and the rolling hills of old brick houses with their chimneys that no longer smoked.

This place meant something to me. It was my grandfather's home before he'd left to go out and forge his own life. I was only just starting to realise that his hard work and struggle, and then that of my own father, had gifted me the opportunities I had in my life. Which were many. The biggest gift was that I had a choice about the life I wanted to live. Looking out across Edinburgh, the strength of these men gave me strength.

I also knew that I was in love. Kaitlin and I had been so guarded that last night in Alicante. We'd even joked about the lives we would go on to lead without each other. But I wanted to live a life with her. I'd been so lovesick as I walked the Munros of Scotland, a deep heartache in my chest that I thought would go away but it never did. A feeling I'd never felt for this long. We'd not talked since I'd left, and from my side it had been too hard to. To know that this amazing girl lived so far away. A different world. A different life. For all I knew she'd forgotten about me, like I'd forgotten about other girls I'd met in my travels. She probably already had a new boyfriend.

I was ready to do good in the world, and I was starting to get clearer on what that looked like. I had just under three years left in the navy. I'd be out at sea for much of that time, doing my job and serving my country like I'd signed up for. But while I moved through those years, I'd study. I already had my eye on two master's degrees, one in international politics and one in international development, focusing on approaches to improve the lives of people living in the world's poorest places. I wasn't burying the memories of Iraq anymore, but I was still horrified by what I'd been part of up there and what was still happening.

And the day I could leave the navy I'd be off. I'd move somewhere and start helping. Maybe somewhere in Africa, where the need felt greatest, and a place I'd never been, and that if I was honest still scared me.

I closed my journal and stood up, looking down the cliff to the empty valley below. My eyes closed, I stretched out my arms wide, the wind buffeting me, and took a deep breath of cold air.

Then with every fibre of my soul, I roared across the valley. A barbaric yawp.

I roared for the men who had made me, and the sacrifices they had made for me.

I roared for the pain I had been holding on to for so long.

For the life I had almost lost so many times.

For the good I still needed to do in the world.

For the life that Kaitlin and I might build together. The children I could picture us having, naked little ones running along a beach somewhere, with her blonde hair and my curls.

I roared for me.

And then, wiping away my tears, I smiled.

***

I'd walked down that afternoon from Arthur's Seat back to my hostel and then paid for some time on the computer in the lobby. I'd confirmed my flight back to Australia, checking the dates and planning my way down to London to make it. Then I'd looked at the two master's degrees I'd been considering and enrolled in them both, emailing Apples and seeing if I could inspire him to do the same. He'd emailed straight back that he'd enrolled as well. It would be good to see him in the new year.

And then I'd emailed Kaitlin. I told her that I wanted to see her again, and asked if she felt the same.

She did.

We'd agreed to meet in Ireland, the last stop for her before she flew back to San Francisco.

***

Now, sitting alone, I swirled a shot of whiskey around in my glass. Temple Bar was coming to life, and the cheerful hum of the Irish drinking filled the street, a Dublin fog already ringing the lamps.

I wasn't quite sure yet what I would do when I saw her. Maybe I would run up like in a Hollywood scene and we'd kiss; the camera spinning around us, a string section reaching its crescendo as our lips met. Or I could play it cool, offer to take her bag, and keep things in the friend zone if that was what she preferred. We'd been careful in our emails since I'd connected in Edinburgh, neither of us giving much away. I reached into my pocket and pulled out an email she had sent me that I had printed. I re-read the final words slowly, the black ink already dulled by the countless times I had folded and unfolded it.

> *"La corazon tiene razon que el razon no entiende." (The heart has reason that reason doesn't understand…)*

And then she walked in. Just a lone girl, pushing the door open and stepping confidently inside. Independent and open to the world. She wore a small backpack on her shoulders, and I knew that inside would be her journal, a vintage copy of Pablo Neruda poems, her CD Walkman and those bohemian dresses she liked to wear. She wore a black woollen hat, and her blonde hair fell out from under it. Gorgeous.

But time alone in the Scottish Highlands had taken away the bluster I'd had in Spain, and I wasn't feeling brave. I took a breath, stood up, adjusted my jeans and sweater jumper and headed over to her. A group of lads had turned around to look at her but went back to their drinks as she saw me and headed my way. Disappointingly I could only manage a kiss on each cheek.

"Hey, how are you doing? Let me grab your bag."

"I'm good. Tired," she replied as she slid the backpack off her shoulders and then rolled them, no doubt stiff from a day of travel on budget airlines.

We slid into the leather booth where I'd been sitting and she let out a big sigh, followed by a little laugh. She really was tired.

"Can I get you a drink?" I asked, wondering if we were going to be this polite and distant for these next few days we had together. She must have a boyfriend; I started to rack my brain as to who in Alicante it might be.

"Just a water would be great."

Cool, just a water, I thought. In Spain she'd always been up for a beer and a talk, or a tequila if she wanted to dance. I didn't know what she wanted to do now. While I nursed my last nip of whiskey, she sipped at her half pint of water I'd poured from a jug at the bar. We descended into devastatingly small chat. About the bus trip. How the weather had been in Alicante recently. The gossip from the clubs. I started to wonder if this had all been a big mistake. I couldn't bear the thought of spending four days like this.

"Do you want another whiskey?" she asked.

"Ah sure; I'll grab it, though."

"No," she smiled, as she put her hand softly on my arm. "I'll get it."

She walked up to the bar, and I looked up at the screen, a replay of an Ireland and All Blacks rugby game. It was dark outside now, and the bar had filled with people. A musician with an acoustic guitar started to play folk songs in the corner. I looked around to try to spot Kaitlin and saw her surrounded by the same group of guys who had watched her walk in. A flash went off, and for a moment she was lit up, smiling sweetly and holding up two small glasses of whiskey. She came back to the booth shaking her head and laughing.

"What was that all about?" I asked as she passed my whiskey to me.

"They think I'm Keira Knightly from *Love Actually*," she giggled and clinked her glass to mine. "It might be this hat; that or they are very drunk."

As the alcohol started to disarm us, she started to slide in closer to me. Our denimed thighs touched first, then, under the table, our pinky fingers. I looked down at our hands. Mine were scarred and weathered, cuts and scrapes picked up from underwater dives, boarding missions and fights. *Too beaten up for a twenty-one-year-old*, I thought. But then her pretty, delicate, thin fingers interlocked in my own. I had a surge of wanting to protect her, care for her, to make sure she was always loved. But I felt that same strength from her.

"Should we get out of here?" I asked as I clinked the mostly thawed ice cubes in my Jameson. I didn't have a plan for what was next; all I knew was that I had a room rented across the river.

She nodded and waved her palm across her whiskey, signalling she was done.

We put on our winter coats and headed for the door, the outside bracingly cold. Hand in hand, not saying anything, we walked past the crowds of smokers. We crossed the street and walked onto the Millennium Bridge.

Ten steps across. Twenty. Still no words.

I was happy that we were together, but nervous for what was next for us and felt my pulse pounding so hard in my hand that she must surely have been feeling it, too.

It was she who pulled her hand back to stop us, then she turned into me, pushed me back against the railing, and we kissed, her cold hands around my face, like she had done that first night in Alicante.

Tears ran down both of our cheeks. I leaned back, let out a full-cheeked breath of air, and shivered with emotion. Love. Fear. Togetherness.

"This is either the best thing we could have done, or the worst," I forced out of my thin lips.

"Right?" she laughed, wiping her eyes. "What do we do now?"

I had no idea. But right then it didn't matter. At least for tonight, we were together again.

***

For the next four days, we did what every young couple in love would do if they were running out of time together. We walked the streets of Dublin, hand in hand. We lay in the grounds of Trinity College reading poetry. We got tangled up in bedsheets on rainy afternoons, windy nights and frosty mornings. On a bus trip north, to Northern Ireland, we held each other for hours, looking out the window at the winter passing by. In Belfast we walked through the winter markets, and bought each other Christmas cards, then wrote love notes at the wooden bar of a warm pub. At the Giant's Causeway we walked out to the cliffs and watched the wind bluster across the water.

And all too soon, it was our last night together. We were in the small town of Bushmills. For dinner, we shared a bottle of South African wine and bowls of lamb stew with crusty bread made by the lady who owned the inn we were bedding down in. She knocked on our door to clear our plates and told us it would be best if we didn't go out to the pub later. Apparently, there had been some trouble in town that week, and IRA men had been seen walking around that night with pistols. One last night in, just the two of us, warm from the cold outside, seemed just fine.

We lost no hours to sleep, and made love like it was the last time we would ever see each other. We felt our hearts swelling with love as they broke.

We marvelled at the sliding door moments. How we might have missed each other in a world of eight billion people and never met. If she hadn't been born in California, she wouldn't have grown up with the Spanish language all around her. Without a friendly Spanish lecturer sharing a brochure for a study abroad program she would have never moved to the country. She had decided on Madrid, but a fortnight before she left, a friend of her boyfriend had talked her into Alicante. If I hadn't been in Iraq, would I have rebelled against my own military and run away to South America? Without the Spanish I had learned there, would I have had the thought that Spain was where I would head next? Without the trauma I had been trying to find my way through, would the psychologist have signed off on that time away? If I hadn't stopped in that bar that first night in Alicante, a town I was just passing through, I would never have worked in the club. If I hadn't gone to the beach that day, I would never have seen Kaitlin. If we had children one day, they would exist because we somehow came together.

We only had a few hours left before she needed to step into the cold, board a bus to the airport, and fly to the other side of the world and back to university. Sitting wrapped in each other, her thighs soft and warm around my waist. She ran her hair from side to side across my face. I closed my eyes and soaked up this sensation that I would miss so very much.

I had never said this to anyone before in my life, but I said it to her. "I love you."

Our lips came together for a deep, slow, long kiss and then she leaned back, moving a strand of my long, curly brown hair away from my eyes.

"I love you, Aaron Tait."

PART 3

PEACE

- THIRTEEN -

FINALLY, WE WERE in Africa. Kenya, to be precise.

Kaitlin's right hand was, once again, interlocked with mine. Her left was held by Mercy, a six-year-old girl from the orphanage, who was barefoot and dressed in a clay-red dress that had once been pink. Walking towards a dusty red square, in the village of Makuyu, we had drawn a crowd, attracting some of the village drunks, some stray dogs and a dozen children who skipped, ran and spun around us. "*Mzungu*, how are you?" they asked repeatedly, pinching their noses to recreate the high-pitched nasal American voices they had heard on the radio.

We are fine, thank you. And how are you? Quite fine. How are we? We are still fine. And them? Very fine.

It felt so good to have arrived. Like we were finally going to be useful after all the university papers we'd written and the endless conversations we'd had.

I was out of the military. Apples and I had been the first from our class to be qualified in our specialisations, eager to get it out the way and focus on the studies we were doing after hours. I then provided valuable service at sea to the mine clearance unit as a warfare officer, diver and navigator. I didn't love the work, but I got it done. And I knew that when I had a goal, of getting through these years and then heading to Africa, I could suck anything up. Apples and Kel were continuing on to complete the full Special Forces course.

At my going-away party, I was gifted a beer glass with my ship's shield emblazoned on it. I drank from it that night, and then left it on the bar.

Now I'd come to Africa to even the ledger. My actions in Iraq had contributed to the deaths of half a million people and to date, I'd tangibly helped exactly zero people in need, save for a few donations to charities and my attendance at peaceful foreign-aid marches. Kaitlin was well ahead of me, transitioning every café at her university to Fair Trade coffee, building homes in Mexico with Habitat for Humanity and volunteering in Mexican American communities in California.

After Ireland, she had moved back to San Francisco to finish at university. A world away from each other, we had spent the next year and a half emailing hundreds of short notes, sending mix CDs burned with love songs and racking up big phone bills. She would call me as she walked home tipsy from college parties. I would write long letters during huge storms at sea. Half a year into our long-distance relationship, we had met in a village on a remote Fijian island, halfway between the United States and Australia. We spent two blissful weeks making love in our thatched hut, hanging out with the village kids each afternoon and swimming in perfect turquoise water. Half a year later, I took annual leave from the navy and flew to America to meet her parents, a friendly and successful couple who welcomed me openly. Not allowed to share a room at her family home as we weren't married yet, we then travelled to New York to be alone. We rented a cheap hotel room in Chelsea and made up for lost nights. We shared plates of pasta in Little Italy and kept warm with coffee refills in diners.

But the real reason that we chose New York was to visit the United Nations. I juggled my navy work with the two master's degrees I was studying, and my fascination, bordering on obsession, to be an international development worker grew exponentially. And the UN headquarters in Manhattan was the epicentre of all this, the place where the big decisions were made. If I were ever going to make a difference at scale, I thought it would be here. Kaitlin's studies were steering towards education, and she would score High Distinctions on essays she wrote about national initiatives across African countries to improve literacy, early childhood support and the livelihoods of young girls. Our plan was to move to Africa to complete a few years at the grassroots of poverty, and then one day we'd be back here in New York, leading things right at the top.

On New Year's Eve when we kissed at midnight in Times Square, we set a resolution that within the year we would be living together. We made that real by August, swapping long-distance phone calls and emails for lying in each other's arms in my Kirribilli apartment, so close to the water that waves lapped up on the windows that were filled with a view of the Sydney Opera House across the bay. Apples lived next door, and as gang of friends we swam in the harbour at sunset, worked on our college degrees late each weeknight, and on weekends, fuelled by cheap red wine, we danced until the sun came up in the thrillingly notorious nightclubs of Kings Cross. If I ignored the weeks I was away at sea, and the feeling of counting down the days until I could leave the navy, it was a blissful, wonderful time with Kaitlin in Sydney. She loved the city, feeling a sense of carefree curiosity and peace that she'd not felt in America for a while. When I was away, she kept herself busy with her education studies, jogs around the harbour and working at a local café where she broke hearts every morning, giving admirers their coffees but not her phone number.

Through this time the world tore itself to pieces as bombs exploded in London, Bali and of course across Afghanistan and Iraq. Kaitlin, Apples and I became increasingly radical in our politics. On a night that President Bush had scheduled a dinner with the Australian prime minister – a neighbour three doors down – we decided to make them a welcome sign. With Bush's boat approaching, Kaitlin welcomed her countryman by pressing play on the Motown song "War", which blared out at full volume from my stereo, drowning out the American anthem being played by the official welcoming band. I then unfurled our sign, which had been disguised to look like a curtain – a queen-sized bed sheet with the words *Bush + Howard: War Criminals* written across it in huge letters with black insulation tape. With some symbolism, I'd strung it up with the laces of the boots I'd worn in the Persian Gulf. But I knew deep down that these flashes of protest in Australia wouldn't make the difference we really wanted to make.

So, after receiving my final paycheck from the navy, Kaitlin and I sold up everything we owned and handed back the keys to our apartment. We booked a one-way flight to Kenya, the one place we could get to with the frequent flyer miles we'd saved up, and found an orphanage online, a place in Makuyu village where we could volunteer and stay relatively cheaply. Beyond these first four weeks, we had a loose plan to find humanitarian jobs somewhere in Africa, but we didn't know how to do that. The continent was massive, and in our first days in Nairobi the city felt overwhelming, like we didn't know how to get a foothold and actually do something useful. Kaitlin's parents in Chicago were nervous for the life that she was choosing to lead and wary of how different it was from their own. Her mother sent us security briefings from the US government, while her father sat down with me and said, "Please keep my daughter safe."

We'd heeded their warnings, but since we'd arrived in Kenya, it had been hard to wipe the grins off our faces. We were thrilled to be there, and we were trying to be useful where we could, working in the garden, cleaning the orphanage and spending time with the children.

As we walked into the markets, we saw smiling stallholders who had laid out their wares on muddy canvases. Bunches of *sukuma wiki* greens to be paired with bowls of *ugali*. Small mounds of glossy local tomatoes. Straw hand brooms for sweeping out huts. Cheap buckets for water, thin cooking pans from India and cheap radios from China. A Swahili pop song shrieked from a PA system, duelling with the microphone held by an over-trebled preacher who chanted threats of damnation, slapping his Bible on his thigh with every mention of Jesus (pronounced *Jeeeezus*). The afternoon sun reflected off the tin roofs straight into the square, which was already a spicy casserole of rotting fruit, body odour and banana wine. We were there to buy supplies for the orphanage. Potatoes. Bags of flour. Sukuma. Dried green grams. Soap. Salt. We tried to purchase a different product from each stallholder to share the budget across the community but still negotiated the best price possible with the little Swahili we had picked up. Young men were hired to cycle the stores two miles back home. My black rugby shorts were filthy, and my old mine clearance branch t-shirt was sweated through. It was an outing not for the claustrophobic, nervous or squeamish.

The preacher finished up his sermon abruptly and, following a spine-tingling blast of high-pitched feedback, the voice of a journalist blared across the square. Someone was holding the church's microphone up to their radio. The din of the market fell quiet and people listened in carefully.

"Only a matter of minutes ago, an official release was handed down from the government stating that President Mwai Kibaki has been formally announced as the winner of the Presidential election. He will be addressing the nation shortly and we will be standing by to bring you all the latest from Nairobi on this most historic of days."

The market broke into cheers, plastic bags flying into the air, people hugging each other with delight and grasping the hands of those around them. The village was a Kikuyu stronghold, the dominant ethnic group in the country, and they were ecstatic that their man had been reelected. I was fascinated; this was history playing out in front of me. The kind of thing I'd read about in papers, but now I was living through. I looked over at Kaitlin and she nodded and smiled weakly. She looked like she was hot, a sheen of sweat across her face. I was hot, too, and the party kicking off in the market wasn't helping things.

I was surprised that President Kibaki had won and wondered if some people would think the election had been stolen. His voice came over the radio a few minutes later, promising prosperity and progress for all Kenyans, before declaring a public holiday for the next day to celebrate. *Bad move*, I thought, picturing the losing majority of the country taking to the streets in protest. It was time to head home to the quiet and safety of the orphanage – an excited crowd always brought some risk with it.

As I swung the last bag of potatoes onto a bicycle, I felt Kaitlin touch my arm. It was something she had done a thousand times, so I thought nothing of it, paid the cyclist his delivery fee, and then looked at her. I was shocked to see her usual Californian tan replaced by a clammy paleness, her fringe matted with sweat against her forehead.

"Hey, what is it?" I asked tenderly.

She started to mumble, and then her eyes rolled back in her head.

"Whoa whoa whoa! What's – " I began. I held her chin gently and tried to get her to focus. "We're good, Kaitlin; you're okay. Just look at me," I heard myself saying, but I wasn't sure if she was.

Then she collapsed.

Fuck, fuck, fuck.

I picked her up, cradled in my arms, her legs hung limp.

A growing group of onlookers had crowded around us, more concerned than curious.

Beyond them was Mansur, a man we'd met on our first day in town. Once Kenya's most notorious drug dealer, and now a humble tea-shop owner since he'd been released from a long prison sentence, he still held some sway in town. Kind people cleared a path for us, and as we approached, he hobbled down the steps of his store, his bone-thin, eighty-year-old arms gripping onto Kaitlin to do what he could to help. As I lifted her up the concrete steps, he called for customers to clear a table, and a group stood up, holding their plastic plates of *mandazi* and their cups of sweet milky chai. Easing Kaitlin down into a plastic Coca-Cola chair, I squatted in front of her. Her eyes would open for a moment and then roll back into her head. I'd been in plenty of first aid situations before in the military, giving people CPR, dressing open wounds and responding when people passed out from exhaustion and heatstroke. But when it is the love of your life, it's different. I was breathing heavily through my nose.

"Kaitlin, I'm right here; can you tell me what's wrong?" I held her face in my hands, but she didn't respond, her eyes still not seeing. Her forehead was hot, but her hands were cold and clammy in my hot sweaty hands. One of Mansur's waitresses brought over a cold bottle of water, and I wet my hand and dripped some onto her head, then held the bottle near her mouth, letting just a tiny amount come to her lips. She opened her eyes, swallowed slowly and mumbled that she felt bad. I felt for her pulse, but it was far too weak to detect.

I breathed out twice to gather my thoughts. There was a small pharmacy in town, but it was likely closed for market day, and the closest thing to a hospital was forty minutes away, with a line of patients who might be in worse shape than Kaitlin. I rubbed the top of her limp hand with my thumb and kept telling her she would be okay.

We certainly weren't the main event, the crowds still celebrating their election win, but Kaitlin was my total focus. And before I thought about what our plan might be if the country went to chaos after this result, I needed to keep Kaitlin alive.

"Mansur!" I yelled above the roar of the crowd. He would know what to do. "Kaitlin needs a doctor!" He helped us outside and called over a bicycle taxi, giving him instructions in Swahili. I sat on the back metal seat and helped Kaitlin on as she slumped weakly up against me.

"Be careful, son. Kenya is about to get very messy."

I nodded to him, unable to process what that meant for us, and our bicycle started off down the dusty street.

The public clinic wasn't open, but a pharmacist gave us an envelope of aspirin and advised Kaitlin to take two every four hours. She barely slept a wink through the night, fluctuating between uncontrollable shivers and hot sweats. I lay in bed holding and watching her, worried she had something aspirin couldn't fix. She finally fell asleep in the very early hours of the morning. She was sick. The worst I'd ever seen her. Kenya was about to descend into madness on the back of a stolen election. We'd been in Africa for a week.

***

She shivered through the night and the next day sweated through the sheets on the filthy single bed we shared. I stayed awake to care for her, planning what we would do if she got worse. I thought of her father and how I would break the news to them if she got sicker. I thought for one short moment what I would do if she died in that room but swallowed down that speculative grief in an instant. I never wanted to go there.

But to my great relief, the fever broke, and it would be just the first of many mystery illnesses we would endure over the next few years. She slowly regathered her strength, eating dry biscuits, taking small sips of water and three days later stepping out of our hut into the orphanage. It was made up of a small compound of stone buildings on a big, red plot of land surrounded by bright green avocado and mango trees. One building housed fifteen children, and there was a smaller building where all the staff and volunteers lived, a small number now that many had left following the violence. A pit toilet served as the bathroom facilities for everyone, and a smouldering hole in the ground at the corner of the property was the rubbish disposal system. A small structure with two iron sheets as a makeshift roof was the kitchen. The well had dried up, so water was a ten-minute walk away.

The illness had scared Kaitlin, but demonstrating a courage that would blow me away many more times, she began to focus her attention on the twenty children. Their lives were made up of a litany of tragedies. Parents who had died of AIDS, heart attacks and cancer. Time spent on the streets. Abuse.

The orphanage they called home was a classic voluntourism program, run by a Kenyan who wore nice clothes and drove a suspiciously nice car. Westerners like us paid to volunteer and were put to work on basic tasks that should probably have been performed by locals for a salary. It wasn't a perfect setup for us, and we felt like with our degrees, and with my military experience, that we were overqualified to be volunteering there but it was a start. We'd find something better soon, as we couldn't afford to keep paying to help. We had a few thousand dollars saved up in a bank account, but at a few hundred dollars a week to volunteer that wouldn't last long.

But we were surprised when that "something better" didn't eventuate. Before we left for Kenya, and then in our first weeks there, we emailed our CVs to nonprofits across Africa. We believed, with a heady mix of naivete and – although we didn't see it yet – privilege, that it would be easy to find work with an international charity in East Africa. We were two young, well-travelled, passionate individuals with six degrees in economic development, social justice and education between us. We'd assumed that organisations would be excited to have us join their teams. But we'd received no replies, not one. We were so passionate to make a difference and had pangs of frustration and disappointment that nobody else seemed thrilled that we turned up.

Undeterred, we kept sending emails and began to do what we could at the orphanage. Breakfast was a cup of sour porridge. Lunch was a small bowl of *githeri*, a mix of kidney beans and hard maize kernels that our Western stomachs would perform somersaults trying to digest. And for dinner, *ugali*, a mix of maize flour and water, was served with half a fistful of *sukuma wiki*, the local spinach.

We would wake at sunrise as the roosters crowed and help the children into their uniforms for school, which was down in the village. During the day the local staff would think up tasks to keep us busy, cleaning the rooms, burning the rubbish or collecting firewood but usually by late morning everything had been done.

So, drawing on her three degrees in education and psychology Kaitlin started to create literacy sessions for the children at night. She spent her days at the local school, trying to help as a teacher's assistant, but mostly having her white skin and blonde hair touched by the community kids as they pinched their noses and asked, "*Mzungu*, how are you?" She brought a humility to this work; her teaching experience was limited to the short placements she'd done as part of her degree.

I spent my time working in the *shamba* to try to improve crop yields and bring some more money into the orphanage to unshackle them from the voluntourism program. I also began to think about what could be done to help families beyond the orphanage to bring more money into their homes.

All the while, Kenya had ripped itself to pieces around us. The post-election violence spread around the country with reports of overturned and burned out *matatus* on the highway near Thika. This was a little too close for comfort, only twenty minutes' drive away by public minivan. Forty people had been locked into a church in nearby Kiambaa and burned alive. Millions of people were internal refugees and thousands of Kenyans had been killed by other Kenyans, with a staggering brutality.

Most of the foreign volunteers, a mix of North Americans and Europeans, had left in the days after the violence started. But after a late-night whispered discussion in the privacy afforded by our mosquito net, we had decided to stay. We hadn't come all this way to leave so quickly. And also, it was Kikuyus who were being targeted in some of the most violent killings, and most of the kids at the orphanage were Kikuyus. We didn't think it was right to run away from them. The violence had surrounded us by then anyway, closing off most escape routes. Commercial airlines were no longer flying out of the airport, and all the major roads were too dangerous to travel on. Kaitlin had called the US embassy to check in, but she was made to wait for an hour before our phone credit ran out. I managed to get through to the British embassy who picked up on the second ring. After a short chat where I said we were staying, the desk officer said simply, "Good for you, best of luck." I'd hung up and got back to work digging a hole for the banana trees we'd been planting that day.

- FOURTEEN -

"AARON, YOU READY to go?"

Asha's bike squeaked and tinkled its way towards me, the long train of her bright yellow kanga skirt tied into a ball to help her cycle more easily.

"Born ready, sister!" I picked up my bicycle, pushed off the dirt for momentum and then slung my leg over the bar.

A young, gregarious Kenyan woman, Asha was in her early twenties and loved by all. She was one of the best volleyball players at the orphanage and led the children's church service every Sunday. The official community worker, her job was to ride her bike around the nearby villages and talk with the grandmothers of orphans that were looked after in foster homes, providing assistance where she could in the form of food, blankets and school uniforms. HIV/AIDS had ravaged this area of Kenya, and an estimated two in every five people were infected, often the young mothers and fathers, who then left behind a generation of children and their grandmothers. Many hardworking, wise and generous old women, whose phase of life called for rest, instead found themselves with as many as ten mouths to feed.

The roads we cycled on were the bright red of volcanic soil, and the forest and maize fields a sea of vivid green. After half an hour of cycling up and down the steep central highland hills,

Asha and I stepped off our bikes and walked down a thin dirt path through dense green. "Mary Njoke's place," said Asha. She wiped the sweat from her face. "You'll love her; she's very strong." As we walked down the path, she let out a loud and high-pitched "*yoop*", and from farther down the valley, a "*yoop*" came in response. We followed the crunching of someone moving through the forest, and Mary emerged from the green. "*Mûrîega?*," she yelled up to us in Kikuyu, using her local dialect rather than Swahili.

"*Ni kwega*," Asha replied, shaking hands with her.

"*Wî mwega?*" she asked as she looked at me with a wide smile, a purple, green and yellow satin scarf tied around her head.

"*Ni kwega*," I responded, holding out my hand, playing my part in the regular exchange of greetings. Mary swung hers out wide and hit my palm perfectly, with gusto. Her grip was strong, callused hands testament to seventy years of farming in her family *shamba*. Hobbling away, she invited us into her home, a mud hut with a dirt floor, no electricity and a bucket for water, and she began to make tea from a wood stove in the corner, cleaning cups for us and sending away one of the children for *mandazi* donuts that we certainly didn't need. While she got to work, Asha casually discussed the health of the children in Mary's care and, in her little notebook, kept carefully written records. She sometimes translated for me, and I just smiled and nodded, not feeling like it was my place to add anything.

As the conversation continued, Mary got on to her family history and how her grandfather had been arrested by the British as part of the Mau Mau rebellions. Asha translated for me.

"She said that the British said to her grandfather that he had to farm a certain way. The English way of just one crop in straight, not the Kenyan way where we plant many things."

This fascinated me. The British sent people to jail for the way they farmed? She spoke about how they had joined the Mau Mau and fought with them. And how they had terrified the British.

When I asked about the Kenyan way of farming, she gave me a local science lesson which Asha shared with me.

"All of the plants, they talk to each other and help each other. Some need nitrogen so they take it from the soil. Others give nitrogen to that very soil. Some plants will kill the bugs and disease so they can be very helpful. If you plant just one crop in those straight rows, you lose all of this benefit."

It was brilliant.

She told us how after her children had died, she had taken on full responsibility for her grandchildren, as well as three orphans from the community. I was amazed by her. She was a Queen. A beacon of love, optimism and wisdom in this tough place. She asked for nothing and instead gave us all she had. Sitting down on a small three-legged stool and sipping the tea she had prepared for us, I wondered if there was anything that I could do for her – whether any of those economics essays I'd written for university had any ideas in them that were of any use here. Or if the ideas from my textbooks were as flawed as the British forcing her grandfather to change his farming approach. But maybe if I merged her thinking with mine, we could do something great. We could help some people. I could help her. Like a karma swap, I'd made Farooq's life worse in Iraq, but I could help Mary here in Kenya.

Later that day, as Asha and I cycled back to the orphanage, I began to ask her questions. "So how much money would Mary have in a week? How does she look after it?" My handlebars juddered down another red dirt road. Picking better lines on the road than me, she told me that Mary and her family would eat mostly food she farmed herself. Any extra money relied on what the maize crop we'd walked through would sell for. If the harvest was bad, it meant very little money, and she would keep it for her family rather than selling in town. And many of the harvests had been bad in recent years.

As we started on another hill, Asha told me that sometimes a farmer like Mary would sell some *sukuma wiki* greens by the roadside and make five extra dollars in a good week. Any money she could save she would tie up in her kanga skirt. The uphill climb took the wind out of our lungs, and we stopped talking.

***

A month later, our second in Kenya, I woke to torrential rain pounding onto the thin sheet metal panels above us. The end of our blanket was soaked, and I made a mental note to patch the roof when it was dry. It was safer in Thika now after the former UN Secretary-General Kofi Annan had helped to sign a peace deal so it would be easy to get the supplies. I flicked on my small Maglite – the same one I'd used on missions in the Persian Gulf – and looked at my watch: 4:22am.

I quietly eased out of our single bed, careful not to wake Kaitlin, put on my shoes and headed out to the dining hall to light the fire for a morning coffee. Then, sitting down on the concrete floor inside, I looked over my notes. The concept was simple and built upon the microfinance model that had worked so well in Bangladesh. There it was a local idea, created by the Bangladeshi social entrepreneur Muhammad Yunus, the "Banker to the Poor", who saw that the classic Western banks and economic models weren't working for billions of people at the bottom of the pyramid.

As the little posters I'd made up showed, if these women could save the local equivalent of $1 a week for the next year, I would personally top them up with a 10 per cent interest rate, money I didn't have to spare but that I was excited to invest. The next poster showed all the little $1 blocks building a big symbolic wall of savings, which they could use to start a business, provide for an emergency or, if they liked, join a pig farming cooperative we were starting, shown on poster three. For this option, we could provide the savers with a female piglet, feed, injections and a friendly male piglet for a sexy visit when the timing was right (not shown on the poster). With the average sow producing twelve piglets in a litter, this meant a $500 windfall each time, more than doubling their household income and putting very useful new money into their family. We had a slightly more expensive goat option, too, which would provide both baby goats and daily milk that could be sold, a $1,000-a-year boost.

After weeks of sharing the idea with women like Mary across the nearby villages, signup day had finally come around, and with it our attempt to launch our new community bank. I'd prepared as best I could, handwriting a short speech, and Kaitlin and I manually created little deposit notebooks for any willing customers. We'd bought biscuits and tea for any attendees and borrowed chairs from the nearest church. Sitting on that concrete floor, I felt like a kid on the first day of school. Of course, I'd written plenty of essays about these ideas and read all the books my professors had assigned, but now here I was in Africa, trying to encourage a handful of old women that this was an idea that could turn their lives and their community around. There were no grades up for grabs here, no comments in red pen on the side of the page. This was real life. A fail meant that they and their grandchildren would go hungry the next year. A pass meant that their lives were that little bit easier.

At 10am, the official starting time, the room was empty. Outside, the rain was still pouring, sheets of water flooding off the verandas and leaving deep grooves in the red clay below. I waited another two hours, and by midday, still alone, the doubting voices in my head were loud. I sat on a table at the back of the room by myself, trying to find some positives in what was starting to look like a total failure. I wondered if the idea was not relevant to their world. Or whether they just didn't trust me. Maybe they weren't fans of pork or goat milk?

When Asha popped inside, I asked her, trying to hide the disappointment in my voice, why she thought things hadn't worked out, and she told me, "*Subiri kidogo*", or have a little patience. So I checked over my speech. Readjusted the stack of deposit books. Stoked the fire to keep the teapot warm, just in case someone did arrive. But another hour passed, and soon the rain had cleared up, and the sun was out again, steam rising from the red mud. Still no-one. For years I'd built myself up to a moment like this. A chance at retribution. A chance to do something positive in the world. But it was flop, and all the optimism and the passion I had couldn't match the feeling of failure I had as I sat there, waiting for no-one.

Kaitlin arrived back from Thika town, where she was checking emails, and kicked off her rubber sandals, which were caked with thick mud, and then stepped inside and sat next to me on the table, her legs swinging. With no-one else in the room, and a rare moment of privacy for us, she kissed me, her mouth sweet and moist with the mango she'd probably snacked on in the *matatu* ride home.

"How was the meeting with the women?" she asked.

"Absolutely no-one showed up." I feigned nonchalance. "So much for these," I said, setting aside the savings books we'd written up by hand, which suddenly looked silly and childish.

"I'm sorry. You worked hard on this." She put her hand on my thigh. "But in good news, we have a job offer!"

I tried to get out of my funk enough to listen. She told me about the school, which was fifty kilometres north of Dar es Salaam, in Tanzania. It offered free high-school education for orphans and at-risk kids. This sounded more like *she* had a job offer, rather than *we*, but I was happy for her. She'd expressed doubts since we'd been in Kenya about where she could fit in and be helpful, whereas out of old military habits I'd found plenty of handyman projects to keep myself busy with around the orphanage. She was excited. This was good for her.

"They say that the project 'literally lacks direction'," – she made air quotes with her fingers – "and that they need a project manager who understands education and development. They're asking if we want to be that project manager, together. They like your leadership skills from the military, and they like my education degree, even though I told them I've only actually taught a class of six-year-olds for not even half a term. They say they'll give us both a hundred dollars each month and a place to stay. They want us to start straightaway."

The more she spoke, the better this sounded. A job like this meant we'd be paid to work, rather than us paying to work. We'd be able to stay longer. Our Kenyan tourist visas were running out and we would struggle to renew them without a job. This organisation in Tanzania would be able to help us secure working visas there. It also gave us the chance to step up. To be seen no longer as idealistic kids with well-meaning degrees but instead to be real humanitarian workers. Also maybe, with the freedom of running an entire community project like this school in Tanzania, we could make a real difference for the kids there. She looked at me and shrugged with indecision.

"What do you think?" Her eyes were shining; this was a perfect match for her passion and studies. And if I was honest, I was excited, too. I shrugged a yes. She smiled and squeezed my leg.

"Let's pack up in here," I grinned, already thinking about the best way to get down to Dar. "The kids can use these notebooks, so they don't go to waste." But then, as I started to gather them together, Asha ran inside and threw out her hand, slapping mine with the usual Kikuyu gusto, her eyes wide with excitement.

"They are here!" she yelled.

"How many?"

"All of them!"

Seconds later a parade of bright kanga-skirted, head-scarf-adorned women bobbed into the room. Kaitlin, Asha and I stood at the door welcoming them all one by one, forty, fifty, then sixty. Big slap handshakes from every one of them.

Asha opened the meeting with a prayer. I felt alive. Inspired. Like I was in exactly the right place, at the right time, doing the right thing, with the right people. I was launching a bank with sixty grandmothers! For the next thirty minutes, we explained how the small bank would work. The women laughed, nodded, tsked and tutted, leaned forward, smiled at children who ran by, gasped, looked out the window, and sometimes clapped their hands. To finish, Asha decided to add a little extra, an impromptu speech from the heart. She was incredible to watch. Twenty-one years old. Proud. Inspired. Sweat glistened on her dark forehead. I couldn't understand her Kikuyu, but she was bursting with passion, appealing to the women to join, her hands excitedly accentuating each point she made. She loved and respected these women immensely, and they gave her their respect in response, reacting to her questions and clapping when they liked an idea. She should run this project, I thought. Not me. Questions flowed for another thirty minutes, which she answered, and then we stopped for a break, passing out bread, cordials, tea, biscuits and bananas. There was a buzz in the room. The women huddled in groups, speaking passionately. After twenty minutes more, we brought things together again.

"If you would like to join the project," I said, holding up my nice pen, which I usually saved for my journal writing, "please take this pen and sign up on these agreements on the table here." I put the pen down on the table with a dramatic flourish. After my long speech, this was my crowning moment.

Asha translated.

And no-one moved.

Not even a scratch at an itchy nose. Some of them stared at Asha; others looked down at the floor. My heart started racing, and I faked a smile, my face beginning to blush. Asha and I looked at each other. We looked around the room. After a long minute, Mary Njoke stood up. Today, she was wearing a bright green kanga, which stretched down to her bare feet, as tough as a mother elephant's hide, and caked in mud from the ten kilometres she had walked that morning. Her beautifully weathered face was framed by her headscarf, under which her hair was cut short. She turned around so that everyone could see her, and then said something loudly in Kikuyu, breaking the awkward silence. The only word I caught was "*mzungu*", the Swahili word for "foreigner". The room exploded into hoots and applause, everyone slapping hands with each other, laughing uncontrollably. I swallowed hard and tried to smile with them. I looked over at Asha for some support, but she was in hysterics, holding one hand to her face. Kaitlin shot me a sympathetic smile and raised her hands in a mutually confused defeat. I knew I was bright red.

"Did you understand what she said?" Asha asked, just getting the sentence out between her laughter.

"Nup," I said shortly.

"She said that she doesn't know how to use your silly *mzungu* pen, but that she is going to join anyway." She laughed, high-fiving me, which brought a new round of laughter from everyone.

I nervously adjusted my rolled-up sleeves unnecessarily and nodded that I understood. We thought we had everything prepared, but I had totally overlooked the possibility that the women couldn't read or write. The awkwardness in the room had been my fault, and for those quiet moments that I was thinking about my own embarrassment, they had been sitting there in their own.

It was Mary who had saved me. I felt silly and excited all in the same breath.

"Okay, Asha, I don't need to do any more speaking, so can you take it from here? Maybe ask them to just raise their hand if they are in." She nodded, still chuckling.

I stepped to the side of the room, held hands with Kaitlin, and watched Asha. My heart was pumping; I could feel it pulsing in my neck, a sensation that usually came to me in moments of fear. But this was different. I couldn't wipe the stupid grin off my face. *This was what change looks like*, I thought to myself. And then something powerful happened. They held hands, all sixty of them, and Mary reached out so that they were all connected to Kaitlin, Asha and me. They all raised their hands together. That beat a signature any day of the week. The bank was open for business, and one thing was clear. I wasn't the person to run it.

Asha was.

And we had to pack our bags for Tanzania. It was sad to leave Kenya, but the banking model relied on a year of deposits from the women to work. I promised I would be back in a year to pay their interest myself, dipping into the few thousand dollars of savings we wouldn't be needing now that we had a $100 a month salary in the new job. I upped the stakes and also promised them that I'd buy all of the women who met their savings targets a brand-new kanga skirt.

We'd also started an experiment in the farm, where I had spent the last few weeks planting. It was a technique that went by the name push–pull farming and had been developed in Kenya. I'd found out about through research online after Mary had told me about her grandfather's farming techniques the British had punished him for. The local team at the orphanage was excited about the approach as well, and we had to wait to see what would happen over the next year as we saw the results of two harvests.

We'd made a good start in Kenya, trying to put aside our Western ideas, and instead listening and adapting to local realities where we could. And leaning back from taking leadership roles, allowing the local team to lean in, felt like the right approach. If we could take this success into Tanzania, we'd do great things.

- FIFTEEN -

THE SWEATING IMMIGRATION officer was quick to stamp my maroon British passport and slide it back to me, but he hesitated when he saw the American eagle stretched across Kaitlin's. He began to thumb through the pages. We were in a border town like a thousand others across the world, with lines of lorries, buses and cars waiting in diesel-clouded queues. Soldiers from Tanzania and Kenya slouched on their sides, assault weapons hanging nonchalantly, and local men hung around suspiciously, watching for travellers who looked tired, weak or foolish enough to pounce on. But besides the usual nerves that came with any border crossing, we were feeling good about Tanzania. The offer of a job and a leadership role was too good to pass up, and we were low on money, and while we weren't going to be making much at $100 a month each, we should be able to manage living in the township on a few dollars a day.

"You are American?" the border guard asked with a thick accent, still looking down at Kaitlin's passport. I wondered if he was a basketball fan and readied to ask him his favourite NBA team. A friend in immigration was going to come in handy if we were to get a one-year working visa.

"Yes, I am," she said politely, clearing her throat nervously and stepping forward to speak through a small hole in the grimy Perspex.

"And what is it you will be doing here in Tanzania?" Still no eye contact. Maybe he wasn't a basketball fan.

I looked over my shoulder to check on the bus. We were the last ones to board, all of the other local passengers already back in their seats. The engine was running, the driver revving it aggressively either to keep it going or send us a message.

"We are travelling to Dar es Salaam," Kaitlin replied.

We had left Nairobi early that morning and had been driving since lunchtime across the Kenyan savannah, complete with running zebras and strolling Maasai herdsmen. But this immigration official wasn't happy. He closed her passport, put it to the side and looked up at her, annoyed.

"And what is it that you will be doing in Dar when you arrive?" Given Tanzania was a largely Islamic country, I wondered if this guy had a bone to pick with the United States, which was still embroiled in the War on Terror.

"We are going to a school," Kaitlin said, smiling as warmly as she could.

"And what will you be doing there at this school?" he said as he held his blank expression.

"Just visiting. Seeing if we can be any help," I replied, leaning into the speaking hole, hoping he still thought highly of my British passport.

"We don't need your help," he said, looking straight at Kaitlin. "Give me your passport back. Just visiting, are you?" He held out his hand, and I apprehensively reached my passport back through the bars and sighed as he crossed out the "six months" on the stamp he had just given to me and changed it by hand to: "*One month. No work.*" He stamped Kaitlin's passport and made the same alteration, and then flung them back towards us.

I tried to politely argue, still optimistic that I could talk our way out of this, but he motioned for us to move on. "Sir, with all due respect, we are not here to cause trouble. But we have paid for a six-month visa," I continued, but he waved us away and raised his eyebrows at the next person, inviting them to come forward. They pushed past us.

Our bus to Dar es Salaam was slowly pulling away from the immigration shed. With no time to argue, we ran towards it, climbed onto the rusted-out steps of the old bus, and found some new seats. Our old ones were taken, and our bags were thrown into the aisle.

"Okay," I said and let out a breath as I sat down and reached for Kaitlin's hand. "Not the warmest of welcomes."

We continued south, burning through the hours by trying to spot animals out the window, gazing at the scale of Mount Kilimanjaro and enjoying some time with just the two of us. At the orphanage, we barely had time away from the children, and at night we shared our room with the other staff and volunteers. It didn't leave much space for romance.

At the Dar bus stop a driver was holding up a sign for us and he drove us through the bustling early evening to a clean, modern and air-conditioned hotel. A note in our room from Margaret, the charity director, told us to relax, order food on her tab and she would meet us in the morning. We couldn't believe our luck, and after all that time in the village, we shared a long shower, soaping each other's bodies and washing off the deep red dirt of Makuyu. We ate a romantic dinner by the beach of fresh fish, salad and wine and retired to our room to make love for the second time that night, in between clean white sheets. Heaven.

We woke the next morning feeling clean, refreshed, well-fed and giddy with excitement that we had landed a job working in international development, a dream for both of us – even if the pay was only $100 a month. I mentioned to Kaitlin that the hotel room would have been four times that amount, but we were happy to accept it, not wanting to look a gift horse in the mouth. We were happy.

Margaret met us for breakfast, a full English with all the trimmings and over frothy cappuccinos began to brief us on our new jobs as the Project Managers of Buka School. A short, pretty and confident Ugandan-born woman in her fifties, she lived in the United States. To us, she was a hero, someone spending her life doing what we wanted to do with ours. But to her, we quickly got the feeling that we were just one more thing on her to-do list before she needed to fly back to the US. Frantic and scattered was the neatest description of her, and over breakfast, Kaitlin and I moved from being amused to bemused. In the car, racing through the city with her driver at the wheel, we just became confused.

"What! Prison! Jesus! Are you serious!" Margaret screamed into the phone. "Oh my God! Is he crazy? We need to …" She flipped her phone shut midsentence, rubbed her face roughly, spoke rapidly in Swahili to the taxi driver, and, with a squeal of its overworked brakes, the long-bullied Toyota Camry swung to the side of the road, pulled an aggressive U-turn in busy traffic, and we were off quickly in the opposite direction.

"Literally, this place just needs some leadership," she said over her shoulder from the front seat as she searched for a contact in her phone. She meant the school. "You guys will be fine," she said, waving her hand loosely in our direction before bringing the phone back up to her ear.

A mile down the road, she slapped the driver on the forearm and pointed at a store, and when he stopped, she was quickly outside, still on the phone and walking into a ramshackle tin hut. She came out two minutes later with a large blue plastic bag, stretched to its limits with okra.

"Best in Dar," she said as she sat down and passed the bag to me, and then motioned at the driver to continue down the street. Minutes later, she slapped the driver's forearm again, and was out, motioning for us to come, so we followed her into a carpentry store, wood shavings on the floor and a dozen sweating Tanzanian men hand-planing planks of cheap blond timber.

"You're gonna need a bed, guys. What do you like?" she asked, not waiting for an answer and instead beginning to negotiate with the owner over the *clack-clack-clack* of nails being hammered. Her phone rang, cash was passed, and we were back in the car once again weaving through thick traffic. The city was huge, and from the back seat, we watched as crumbling colonial cubes, mosques and makeshift tin shanties raced past our windows. Judging by the murals, Osama bin Laden was even more popular here than in Kenya.

A dozen tasks, and some hours later, we pulled up to the police station, a crumbling white building with a crowd of women outside, likely all working to get their husbands, fathers or sons out of jail. Margaret stepped out of the car and stormed up the stairs, beckoning us to follow and yelling, "*Iko wapi Bakari*?" at a policeman who was slumped in his chair, a rifle leaning up against his thigh. He gestured casually to a nearby desk that two officers slouched up against, heavy wooden sticks in their hands. They didn't look at me, but instead leered at Kaitlin, which she noticed and so pulled in closer to me.

"Your sister or your wife?" one of them asked.

"Wife," I lied, a flick of anger surfacing that I thought best to swallow.

"*Iko wapi Bakari*?" Margaret yelled again, hitting her hands together.

"*Subiri kidogo*," one of the officers said with a wave of his hand, taking one more look at Kaitlin as he walked out of the office. But Margaret did not want to be told to "wait a bit", and she started yelling at them in Swahili, flipping open her phone and moving through her contacts. I figured she was going to call someone powerful, and apparently so did the police officers, because one of them stood up and walked into a back room. Margaret walked out to make more phone calls; feeling like we were of little use,

Kaitlin and I found a wooden bench to sit on. We pulled in tight, exhausted and thrown by the day.

An hour later, the officers came out holding a strong young African man by the arm, his shirtless torso glistening with sweat. His blue school trousers were ripped, and blood was smeared across his face, his own, by the looks of his swollen nose. This must have been Bakari. He looked about my age. He was scared. I felt bad for him, and I felt Kaitlin's caring energy surge through her hand. Looking around the room with terrified eyes, his shoulders sank with relief when he saw Margaret standing in the corner near us. But she was not as happy to see him. He was pushed our way and ordered to sit on the dusty concrete floor, where he collapsed into a sobbing heap, his face in his hands. Kaitlin and I didn't know what to do, so we looked at Margaret.

"Bakari, what have you done, silly boy?" she asked tenderly, after a few long seconds. He apologised as he reached out his hand to her, tears streaming down his face.

"Don't say you are sorry; I want to know what you have done," she asked again, this time with a flash of aggression in her voice. She reached into her bag for her phone, which she flipped open and closed again, checking for new messages. He kept shaking his head and apologising.

"Are you going to answer me or just say *pole sana* over and over?!" she snapped at him. He looked up at her, desperation streaked across his face. Then he looked at us. I wanted to say, *Sorry, mate, we are new*, but Margaret stood up from her chair, flipped her phone open and walked out of the station.

The feeling that crises like these would be ours to manage starting tomorrow was unnerving – we felt like we had not been equipped by Margaret for what was coming. In between debating with the police, Margaret explained the story to us: Bakari – one of the older students at the school – had that morning assaulted one of the teachers. The teacher was half his size and had not fared well in the fight. The police were now threatening to lock Bakari up for assault, a position that Margaret didn't agree with. After hours of deliberations, she finally got her way, and we walked out of the station with Bakari and began to make our way to the school, disoriented, hoping for more clarity. Margaret's phone battery had finally died, and desperate to get a briefing from her, we started asking questions.

"Margaret, is it possible for you to tell us more about our role at the project?" I asked, leaning forward from the middle seat, Bakari on my left, Kaitlin on my right. The little car worked its way through snarls of traffic, the dark roads lit only by headlights and roadside fires. "Literally, it just needs some structure, some discipline, some leadership," she repeated. "Try things. We are having some problems with teacher attendance at the moment. Do you know about goats?" she segued.

"Sort of," I answered. "I grew up hunting them, always happy to learn more, though. How many kids are at the school, and what ages are they? The human kids, not the goat kids," I joked, but it didn't land with anyone.

"Oh, hundreds of students, but these teachers don't know how to bring structure. Literally, just some leadership is all the place needs. Wait, did I buy okra today?"

"Yeah, you did; yep, it's back here," said Kaitlin. "And the students, how is their learning going?"

Margaret ignored her and adjusted the charger cord she'd plugged into the car lighter, then flipped her phone open, which didn't light up. She threw it back into her bag, starting up a conversation in Swahili with the driver, a funny one apparently as she exploded with laughter, a sharp slap on her thigh crackling through the car. Kaitlin glanced at me and raised one eyebrow.

"And how many classrooms are there?" I asked.

"The buildings were new recently, but the termites are ..." She reached deep into her bag and then across for the driver's phone, its dull green face lighting up hers. "Like I said, it just needs some leadership there; it's gonna be great. You guys are gonna be great."

We had come to Tanzania in good faith based on a couple of short emails and still had very little idea of what we were going to be doing. In Nairobi, our research in a cybercafé told us that Buka was a "challenging peri-urban settlement" that was "poorly served by international agencies". We learned that the region had one of the highest rates of malaria in Africa and that HIV/AIDS was estimated to be as high as two in every five people. In the military, I was used to getting a good handover before taking over a job, but it was clear that wasn't happening tonight. Margaret swapped her SIM card into the driver's phone, and it flashed to life as she opened it up. Delight on her face.

That was it.

The briefing was over.

"Ask Bakari. He can answer your questions," she said over her shoulder as she typed a number into her phone and put it to her ear. "He is the head boy."

I looked at him, the best student in the school – just out of jail, blood across his face. He smiled a weak smile and held out his hand, which was blood-stained as well. I shook it. All I wanted to do was ask how Kaitlin was feeling about all this, but it wasn't appropriate in front of, well, the head boy.

An hour later, close to midnight, we sat on the concrete floor of what would be our home for the next year, a candle between us. A small plate of dinner had been left for us, which we were deeply appreciative of, and we worked our way slowly through a cold plate of *ugali*, a stodgy mix without taste, and red kidney beans, also without any flavour. In only our underwear, we still sweated, and the humidity, even this late at night, made the air thick, punctuated only by the buzz of mosquitos. The concrete felt good on our bare skin. The bed that Margaret had ordered us earlier that day had been delivered – one single bed fit for a child, the varnish they had slapped on it still sticky and pungent. At least it drowned out the stench of the pit toilet in the corner, a small open hole over it. The windows had steel bars on them, but the door only a comically small lock, something I'd already made a mental note of to get sorted. While I didn't admit it to Kaitlin, driving that final stretch through the slum to arrive at the school, I felt nervous for her safety. Buka felt dark, ominous and intimidating, and while visiting a place like this for a day was one thing, choosing to live here for the next year in a tin shack was another. My greatest fear was that something horrible would happen to Kaitlin. I tried not to think about the what-ifs. While driving into Buka, Margaret had advised us to never walk around at nighttime, never accept a drink from someone we didn't fully trust (as it might be poisoned), and she appeared upset that the school's night watchman appeared to have quit his post. Kaitlin rarely seemed worried in Africa, but I more than made up for it, often feeling on edge and scanning busy markets and bus stations for threats as we walked through them. My knife was already tucked by the side of the bed in case anyone tried to get into our house.

Kaitlin put down a handful of *ugali* and looked at me. "What do you think the chances are that we get any helpful info from Margaret tomorrow?" Still chewing, I looked up at her and reached for our little Nokia 3310. I held up the message that had come through thirty minutes earlier.

Leaving tomorrow early. Good luck! Margaret.

What we did know was that we were the project managers of Buka High School. The buildings were full of termites, the kids barely attended and neither did many of the teachers. Only one student had ever passed the exams, and the head boy had a fresh record of beating up the teachers. I was a young, retired military officer with a few degrees who once ran a bar in Spain. Kaitlin was a graduate teacher with a grand total of five weeks' teaching experience in Sydney. We were twenty-five and out of our depth, but we had a huge amount of passion to try to make a difference; and we had each other. We'd watched the Make Poverty History concerts where Bono and Coldplay had inspired the crowds to change the world, and well, this was what it looked like. It was messy. Hard. If it was easy, poverty would have been solved by now. We weren't going to change thousands of lives here, but we could help the hundred or so kids who attended the school to get an education. It was something.

Kaitlin started laughing out of nowhere. "You know, Aaron, literally – "

And I finished her sentence: "The place just needs leadership!"

In silence, we tried to eat more of our food, Kaitlin giving up one forced mouthful before I did. I wondered if we were both thinking the same thing. Maybe we should have stayed in Kenya. No malaria, mangoes on the trees, and a community inspired to dig in and improve things in Makuyu. I wasn't going to raise it, though; she'd been so excited to put her skills to use here. We'd be fine. We'd work things out.

"Why is this place such a mess?" I asked her. "It sounds like the kids in Buka don't have much. If most of them come from the slums, shouldn't this school be a golden ticket? Free education. A shot out of poverty. Surely, when they hear about this place, they'd be pumped. Like for once they might get a lucky break. But by the sounds of it, when they arrive, it's a bit shit."

"Let's see what it all looks like tomorrow," she said, blowing her fringe up and waving her hand to cool her face. I stood up and leaned against the windows, holding the bars that crossed the tattered flyscreen. Outside, tall palm trees waved slowly in the wind and white sand shimmered under a full moon. All the ingredients of paradise. But it felt like we were a long way from that. Kaitlin came up and hugged me from behind. It was hard to believe that after meeting in a little Spanish town, we were here, years later, doing this. Together. We had that.

- SIXTEEN -

THE QUIETEST OF knocks on our door woke me from a too-short sleep. I pulled my arm out from under Kaitlin and parted the mosquito net that was stuck to the still-sticky varnish on our single bed. I thought of those cappuccinos we'd had the morning before. I doubted we'd be so lucky today.

Pulling my jeans on, I found a creased t-shirt and brushed my hair flat with my hand. Then pushing aside the backpacks I'd put there last night as a makeshift lock, I opened the door. Three young men were sitting on the chipped concrete veranda at the front of our little house and they stood up to greet me. The oldest had the darkest of skin, which shined bright in the morning sun, perhaps helped by a scoop of Vaseline as part of his morning routine. He was dressed well, a nylon jacket with a dragon on it, something that wouldn't have been out of place in *The Lost Boys* film. He reached out his hand to me and as I shook it, he brought his other up, cupping mine with both of his. He spoke quietly.

"Morning. Morning. Welcome to Buka. I am Peters."

Another boy held out his hand to me. He was tall and strikingly handsome, his hair shaved much shorter than Peters, who I now assumed was a teacher.

"*Poa poa*, Mr Aaron, I am Jelani," he said confidently; I caught the street slang he used and felt a flash of pride that I'd understood.

The third boy shook my hand but didn't speak. Jelani introduced him.

"This here is Frank; he is not so good with English." He had an innocence about him; a kindness in his eyes.

Peters spoke again. "We are very happy to help you this morning. Maybe we show you around first."

This was a much warmer welcome than we had received from the immigration official as we had crossed the border into Tanzania or from Margaret the day before, and the doubts of last night began to fade. I thought about waking Kaitlin but decided to let her sleep. Peters asked how long we were staying for.

"I think we are here for a year." I smiled. It felt good to say a year. Like we were really going to have a go at getting something done. I was confident we'd be able to work out the visa situation.

Buka town seemed to merge in with the school's grounds, mostly shanties made of tin sheets and tarpaulins. A sand quarry and a cemetery were on the perimeters, which were unfenced. The classrooms were a concern; many of the timber posts that held up the tin roof on a dangerous lean were termite-ridden. Frank opened a door, but it fell off its hinges and he leaned it up against a wall. Inside the rooms, broken tables and chairs were covered in graffiti. There was no sign of any learning materials on shelves or stuck to the walls.

"How many students study here, Peters?" I asked as walked past the pit toilets, where pools of shit only a foot below the floor slithered a horrifying dance under a blanket of maggots.

"So many, Mr Aaron," he answered. "We have sixty boarders, thirty boys, thirty girls, and we have more than a hundred who live nearby who come for school each and every day."

As we stepped into the boys' housing, I looked up at the chipboard ceiling, which sagged dangerously, riddled with white ants and damp. The small rooms that divided up the larger building were separated by thin plywood, and filthy mattresses were squeezed in tightly together across the floor. The boys were getting dressed for the day, their heads shaved and their white shirts tucked into navy-blue trousers. But none of them seemed as confident as Jelani; and they gave me shy nods as I was shown into each room. The girls' area was off-limits to us, but the guys showed me the farm, which other than rows of weeds consisted of one papaya tree, with one small fruit growing on it. It was a far cry from the lush *shambas* we had farmed in Kenya.

We walked down the hill to the water hole, where there were already twenty students waiting. Peters introduced me to some of them as "Mr Aaron, who will be here for one year, and Sister Kait, too." They nodded shyly and beckoned for me to skip to the front of the line, but I refused, happy to wait my turn, which came fifteen minutes later. "Do you have your bucket?" Jelani asked me, as we stepped up for our water. But we didn't. We were outsiders with no water, no food and no knowledge of the way things worked in this slum. Our belongings extended to a small bag of clothes each, our journals, one torch and my knife. Listening in on our conversation, a teenage girl with a club foot stood up painfully and hobbled over awkwardly to us, her foot dragging through the dust. Her bucket hung by a wire handle that bit into her thin, twisted wrist, and she said a few words in Swahili before motioning for me to take it, a determined look on her palsied face.

"No, I can find a bucket; I don't need to take hers." I looked at Jelani and shook my head, hoping that he could translate for me. She thrust it out again. Recalling a line a friend had shared with me – *a generous act is to accept generosity* – I accepted. "*Asante sana*," I said, bowing my head to the young girl and shaking her twisted hand as I introduced myself. She told me her name, Zuri, Swahili for "beautiful", then rubbed her face and hobbled away.

The water hole was different from the open well we'd become used to in Kenya, with its clear, cold water that filled every three-gallon bucket we sent down. Here, it was a thin, white PVC pipe, only a few inches exposed above ground. The students had assembled a ten foot–long bamboo stick with a cup on the end. The technique was to lie down flat and drop the pole as deep as they could, the top of the piping right up under their armpits. Then they pulled the stick all the way out and expertly poured the cupful of brown, particle-filled water into the bucket. Ten or so cups filled a bucket about a quarter of the way up, which was drinking, washing and cooking water for the day.

Frank offered to help and when he was finished, our borrowed bucket was immediately scooped up by Zuri. Hoisting the bucket confidently onto her head, she started up the hill, her foot dragging through the sand. The generosity of these children was astounding to me. Walking the hundred yards up the hill to our small house behind this young girl, so strong in the face of so much hardship, I scanned the school grounds and my spirits continued to rise. I glanced at the overgrown farmland, filled with weeds, and imagined it full of crops ready to harvest. Peering into the empty classrooms through their broken doors, with their broken desks inside, I imagined them full of children, a motivated teacher at the front. People in the slum walked down the path outside the barbed wire fence, and I wondered if we could start a community bank for them like we did in Kenya. Even as I walked up to our small house, surrounded by stones and sand, I imagined what it would look like with a little garden, some purple bougainvillea climbing the walls, and a few chairs out front.

We could do something here.

I pushed the door open to find Kaitlin sitting on the concrete floor in the empty house, unpacking her rucksack of clothes, folding them and placing them on the floor up against the wall. "This place is great," I said. Zuri shuffled our bucket of water over to the corner of the room, I heard a knock and looked up to see Peters again. Apparently, no other teachers had turned up to school that day. He asked me what we should do.

"Ready to teach?" I said to Kaitlin. We splashed a small handful of water on our faces, drank a glass of dirty water for breakfast and, a few minutes later, walked out together towards the classrooms, ready for our first day.

***

We'd moved to East Africa to help solve problems. And in Buka, there were many.

A shortage of teachers was a common one. On our first day, three decided to turn up at 11am, one of them with the sourness of alcohol on his breath. They let us know they were on strike until we provided a bag of sugar for the staffroom – easily solved. But once they started teaching, it wasn't much of an improvement on their absence; their approach was to spend the first thirty minutes of a lesson writing up some paragraphs on the blackboard from an old textbook and then, in the second thirty, have the students write it into their notebooks.

No firewood was another common problem. A short-term option was trimming branches from the trees, chopping them up and drying these to help with the food cooking. The shortage of food was trickier, and we did our best to find the sacks of food with the fewest weevils possible with the limited budget we had. We ate what the students ate, which meant we skipped breakfast. Lunch was a fist-sized lump of *ugali* and a few spoons of kidney beans boiled in water. Dinner was the same. This diet partially filled an empty stomach, but it was low on the vitamins the children needed for their growing bodies. As for water, the well we used on the first day was running dry and the water was certainly not fit for drinking; it was full of particles and more than likely heavily polluted by the rubbish built up all through the township. But with nothing else available, we all drank it anyway. There was rarely electricity. We had almost no money for medicine for the children who were sick.

In the first few weeks, Kaitlin spent her days teaching up to fifty students in one classroom, while I figured out how I could be helpful around the school. To make our little house nicer, I dismantled the single bed and, using some timber I found, extended it to a double. I started a small garden with herbs and vegetables to determine by trial and error what grew, as well as a bougainvillea plant to climb our wall. While we'd started to feel safer, I had followed through with my gut feeling and installed two thick steel bolts across our door, which we locked shut at the end of each long day, usually around 10pm.

A twelve-foot wire antenna I'd fashioned from scrap metal and attached to the top of our roof was bringing in a crystal-clear signal for the BBC World Service, and we'd cheered as Obama had moved up against Hillary in the primaries. Kaitlin and I loved him and had fully bought into his message of hope and change. Indeed, it was inspiring our approaches in Buka.

I'd also been making friends in the township – and when I went shopping, every smallholder was included, so soap was purchased from one store, salt from another, rice from the mama with the Obama kanga skirt, and matches from the man with the Osama bin Laden poster. I'd made a friend at the immigration department in Dar, too, and we had three months added to our visa. I'd lied and said we were taking a Swahili language course.

We'd received almost no new information from Margaret and, other than the small cheque she sent each month for staff salaries and food, it felt like we were on our own.

But we secretly loved the autonomy, feeling like we could get things done and the excitement we felt on our first morning had only risen. Each night we stayed up late talking through ideas for new projects that might raise the children's grades, improve their health and bring more resources into the school. We wanted to start an entrepreneurship program that would see eager students start their own businesses – I would provide a small amount of seed funding from my own pay, just $10 given out each week, but once they paid me back from any sales they made, they could keep all of the profits.

We'd started a fundraising drive on Facebook to build and fill the shelves of the community's first library, pestering our friends and family back home to chip in whatever they could; the price of a coffee was the regular ask. I had a plan for a one-acre farm that would use the push–pull approach as well as chicken business; their droppings were good nitrogen for the soil. Kaitlin had developed a teacher training course for the staff, and an after-hours tutoring program for the students who wanted extra help. I had a microfinance program sketched up for the shop owners in town. I was leading a classroom repair project, with carpentry lessons included for the students. Each idea had its own poster stuck to our wall with a budget, a timeline and who was in charge of what. In the absence of direction, we were running the whole school and seeing it as a beacon of hope for the community. Impatient to get started, I'd visited the town and withdrawn money from our meagre savings, and Kaitlin and I made strategic decisions on where we wanted to direct our money in tiny instalments, $10 here, $50 there. It was all doable if all the staff and the students got involved. We weren't doing things by halves. We'd come to work. To change things.

On top of all of this, we'd set one big goal.

In the school's decade-long history, the furthest any student had progressed was grade 10. With Margaret's support, he had been moved to a nearby high school to support his studies with the hope that he'd make it to university to study architecture. Audaciously, we set a target of ten students passing the national exams this year and moving on to grade 11. We wrote this on the inside wall of our house in permanent marker.

It was all very exciting, and we knew one person would be key to all of this. Edna.

We met her on our third day at the school when she introduced herself as the head teacher. She kept an office at the school that was locked up much of the time, and in the lockable drawer of her lovely, neat desk, she held the school financial records, petty cash and textbooks. For weeks, Kaitlin and I had been eager to meet with her to talk about the school and her role as head teacher and determine how we could work together in the absence of any clarity around our positions. It wasn't that she was busy teaching or in meetings, she just didn't turn up to school all that often. But today, I'd finally secured a meeting.

Dressed up as smartly as I could in my jeans, shirt and desert boots, I walked down the hill to the meeting place, a small food stall in the main street of Buka, easy to spot for its bright orange, Fanta-branded umbrellas. Edna arrived late and made quite a sight as she walked towards me, striding almost six feet tall, fitted out in matching lime-green satin pants, a blouse and a shawl wrapped around her shoulders. She was sweating profusely in the midday sun. She poofed the side of her tall afro with her hands and then wiped her face with a handkerchief before taking a seat.

"Would you like tea or a soda, Edna?" I asked.

"Fanta, please, Aaron. I like it very much." I ordered hers and a Stoney Tangawizi for me. She seemed in good spirits, and I had high hopes for the meeting. But the good vibes didn't last long. Right as the warm sodas were placed on the plastic Coca-Cola table mats by the waiter, we each took a sip, and then she looked straight at me. "Margaret brought you here to fire me, didn't she?"

I swallowed a mouthful of warm ginger beer and tried to laugh politely, leaning back in my plastic chair. In the corner of the room, a television blared loudly, a distorted Tanzanian pop band on the screen gyrating to their latest hit. I noticed several customers at the other tables staring at me, a rare white person in their township.

"No, Edna. I'm not here to fire you. In fact, I've barely heard from Margaret since she left." The nearest cybercafé was an hour's travel away, so we hadn't been online for weeks.

"So why are you now receiving the cheques from Margaret? That was my job," she said, pursing her lips. "Mr Aaron, I heard a rumour that you want to see students going to university. You must know that these students don't want to learn. Besides, you are not a teacher. I am an excellent teacher, and I have taught in the finest schools in this country. Schools with rose gardens, too many teachers, groundskeepers and a staffroom with sugar for tea and cakes every morning. This place, though," she said with a dismissive wave of her hand, "these kids don't care. They are sneaking off, stealing things, beating teachers and having sex. Can you imagine! They are very disobedient, these children. Did you know that they take the desks out to the farm to have sex on! No … these kids …"

She trailed off, shaking her head and tutting, before reaching into her blouse for her handkerchief to wipe the sweat from her face. "No, Aaron, you are not a teacher," she repeated, looking away from me, seemingly more interested by the music playing on the television than our meeting. "And Kaitlin has never taught in this country. Neither of you should be doing any teaching; that is my directive as head teacher." I wondered if she didn't like us because she believed we were a threat to her, or simply because we were outsiders: people who had come into her place who thought they had the right ideas.

She finished her Fanta in one final gulp.

She stood up, signalling the end of the meeting; I'd barely spoken. I left some shillings on the table to pay and we started back towards the school, a few hundred metres away, walking in silence. We tried not to trip on the deeply eroded rivets that had sliced up the path during the monsoon rains and then came up to the front gate of the school, a rotting panel of timber dangling on hinges that were too small.

"We have the mayor coming tomorrow to the school," she said to me as we stepped through it. "You will need to provide sodas for them and some small bites. You can use the money that Margaret sent you."

Our small house was the first building inside the gate. She stopped at the small garden we had planted the week before. Looking down, she pointed her foot at a small twig coming out of the ground. "What is this?"

"That little stick will one day be a beautiful bougainvillea bush." I tried to smile, hoping to at least close our failed meeting on a pleasant note.

"No, it will not work," she said. "At my old school, we had huge, big bougainvillea trees, perfectly trimmed." She tapped the twig with her foot; it fell over into the dirt, and then she walked away, heading towards her office, where three of the teachers were waiting for her. I waved at them, but they turned away.

I was angry. These were staff that barely came to school, apparently led by Edna, who was absent as often as they were. Did they not care about these kids? Were they happy to just receive their pay every month from Washington and see how little work they could get away with?

Across the square, I could see Kaitlin with a packed classroom, her students working in small groups on activities she'd stayed up late preparing. Peters had a class too, both sleeves of his cool jacket pushed up past his elbow. I didn't know how he wore that in the heat. I ran my hands through my hair, knelt down in the sand to replant the bougainvillea and then looked around at the school, wondering how I could be useful. I wasn't looking forward to telling Kaitlin that Edna didn't want her teaching anymore.

I looked at a pile of posts I'd gather up around the property. A job on my to-do list was to build a fence to reduce the number of drunken men walking onto the grounds and threatening the girls. After changing into my shorts and shoes, I grabbed the tools I'd bought with my own money, a shovel, hammer and some nails. I headed off to get to work, but before I dug the first hole, I looked inside to see two of the senior girls sleeping, their heads resting on their arms. I recognised Zuri, who had helped me with a bucket of water on our first day.

"Hey, Zuri," I said, sitting down on one on the desks. "What class should you have now, and where is your teacher?"

She laughed at me, and said, "We are in English class as of now, Mr Aaron. And we are supposed to be studying the book *Things Fall Apart* by Chinua Achebe. Madam Edna is our teacher, but she has not come for a long while."

"Have you read it yet?" I asked. In time I would come to realise I should have read it too. It tells the story of Okonkwo, a warrior who opposes European colonialism and Christian missionaries.

The girls both shook their shaven heads – neatly trimmed in the common student fashion, with the five-cent razor blades for sale in every kiosk in Buka. "Madam Edna has a copy of the book in her office, but she said it is her copy, and she needs it for teaching." Which she hadn't been doing for a while, it seemed.

Patience was not a virtue for me. And in that moment my anger spoiled over. I decided in that classroom that I wasn't waiting to get Edna's support on anything. Kaitlin and I were here to improve the school, and it was time to get to work. Right now. Peters would support us, and even if it was just the three of us we'd turn this place around.

I walked back up to our house and saw Edna's office locked up. She and the three other teachers had left for the day. I interrupted

Peters and Kaitlin's classes and called a school meeting. We announced every learning project that had a poster, including the goal of at least ten students graduating at the end of the year, but put many of the others, like the entrepreneurship program and the community bank, to the side. Now that I would be teaching too, I wanted to focus. We would start classes thirty minutes earlier from tomorrow morning. We all had a lot of work to do.

Later that night, Peters, Kaitlin and I sat on our veranda and had our *ugali* and beans dinner together.

"What did Edna actually say in that meeting?" Kaitlin asked. "You were fired up when you got back." She laughed.

"She was just so negative," I complained. "I was trying to be polite, so I barely got a word in, but in her opinion this place has no chance of ever being good. She didn't want me teaching, which is maybe fair enough given I'm not a trained teacher, but then she said she didn't even want you in the classroom."

"But you still want to teach tomorrow?" she queried, hesitation in her voice.

"Of course. I've got three fucking degrees; I think I can teach grade 8 English and social studies." I put my plate down. The *ugali* was as unappetising as ever.

"But aren't we making things hard for ourselves if Edna is offside? She probably has a point; you've come in pretty hot, Aaron. Maybe we slow things down a bit and – "

But I interrupted her. "No. Honestly, she's full of shit. She barely walks through these gates every week. We don't need her. Right, Peters?"

He stayed quiet for a moment. Always impossibly diplomatic, he'd not upset a single person since I met him. A bit like Kaitlin. I didn't think it was time for diplomacy: it was time for action. If the military had taught me one thing, it was that to get the job done, sometimes you had to upset people.

"Be careful, Aaron," he warned, his voice quiet. "Edna can cause trouble for you. She is friends with the mayor, with many people in Buka. Just be careful."

I shook my head. "I'll be fine, mate. I'm not worried," I said, and laughed thinly. "I'm off to bed. See you in the morning, bright and early." And I tapped him twice on the shoulder.

- SEVENTEEN -

CLASSES STARTED ON time the next day; I made sure of that. But so did the trouble. Beginning with a text message from Edna, informing me that what I'd done was an act of treason, and that the police and the mayor had been notified. She also told me that she and all the staff had quit.

In fact, it wasn't all of them. Peters was staying. He'd been orphaned himself in Rwanda, and he had been supported by Margaret through his own education. I didn't give her text another moment of thought. I felt like I had a job to do. A big job.

We woke every weekday at 5am and, with the students, got to work cooking the breakfast. By 8am we were all in class, and Peters, Kaitlin and I taught lessons all day, until 3pm. Those students that lived in the township would go home, and but with the boarders we would get to work cooking dinner, and on the farm for an hour, trying to grow okra and spinach to supplement the stores we had. There was soccer and games as the heat left the day, and after dark, extra tutoring for those who wanted it. Saturdays were for projects, and we would spend the day repairing fences, roofs, tables and chairs, or building chicken hutches and cleaning up the school. Some of the boarders would help out; Jelani, Frank and Zuri were always keen to hang out with

Kaitlin and me. Peters worked just as hard as we did, and slept in the same humble house as the boys. Our house was tiny, but we made it our own, painting the walls and hosting cups of tea with the students who wanted to spend time with us.

On Sundays we rested, and sometimes made our way to a cybercafé to check email. Asha often shared good news about the bank. Most of the women were saving consistently. The farm was also working, the maize growing tall with the new approach they were experimenting with. I reinforced that we would be true to our promise, we'd be back at the end of the year, but were too busy in Tanzania to come sooner. Kaitlin would read emails from her mother alerting her to security warnings she'd been reading about East Africa, but we would assure her we were safe. And in the late afternoon we would go to our favourite bar. They did two things well.

The first, chips *mayai* – their only dish on the menu – consisted of a plate of potato chips cooked in two eggs, with fried goat meat and chilli on top. A salty, fat-filled delight that was a far cry from what we ate the rest of the week. The second was beer, Kilimanjaro lagers ordered "*baridi sana*", very cold. On this Sunday we'd talked our way out of playing in a soccer game and had snuck away to take a break and recharge for the week ahead. As I clinked my beer to Kaitlin's, one of our old teachers passed by in the street. He was drunk and stumbling, but we picked up some words; that we should "watch our backs" and something about curses.

"Curses," I laughed to Kaitlin. "That's a new life experience to check off."

"Yeah, you laugh," she said and winced, "but that's pretty full on."

"I think you're fine. Everyone loves you. I think all the curses are coming my way." And they did. Kaitlin was never one to rock the boat. She was loving and supportive of the students and hadn't been tainted in the eyes of the old staff the way I had. "I know who the witch doctor is. I'll buy him a beer the next time I see him; see if he can reverse the curse." The alcohol had taken the edge off a bit, so part of me was joking, but I could see Kaitlin was worried.

"Honestly, change is hard. Yeah, we've upset some people, but it's easier without them. We just have to stay the course. We are doing the right thing."

As the day's shadows lengthened, we finished our drinks and headed back to school.

We stepped through the fixed and freshly painted front gate, one of yesterday's jobs, to find Peters sitting out the front of our house listening to the radio.

We sat down on our front stoop beside him, and I groaned like an old man as I did. My bones ached, which I put down to how hard we'd been working recently. Kaitlin sat beside Peters rather than me.

"I've been receiving text messages from Edna that are very bad," he sighed. "The staff have told me that they have now paid for curses to be placed on you, Mr Aaron."

"See, I told you, Kaitlin. You are curse-free." She didn't answer. "Don't worry about all that, Peters. They are just regretting that they quit. We're on track. Me, you, Kaitlin … we're a team." I leaned back on my elbows, the concrete still warm from the day. Then Frank ran around the corner and up to the house, breathing heavily.

"Mr Aaron, the mayor of Buka wants to see you at his home now," he said in between breaths. His English had improved rapidly, helped by our conversations each morning as we collected firewood together. "He is angry, Mr Aaron."

To be honest, before Edna had brought him up at our one and only meeting, I didn't even know there was a mayor. Buka was a collection of tin shacks, hardly a thriving metropolis, and Margaret certainly hadn't mentioned him. Kaitlin and Peters offered to come but, preferring to keep them out of what I expected to be a nasty meeting, I lifted myself up heavily and walked to the mayor's house with Frank, who said he'd show me the way and wait at the front for me. Making my way up the grand driveway, I laughed at the size of his house, an enormous colonial-era manor with balconies on all sides and surrounded by manicured gardens.

Two huge black dogs ran towards me, the fleshy pink of their gums giving way to fierce fangs and long strands of saliva whipping wildly into the air. I turned and shielded my body for a moment, but realising quickly that they could outrun me, I faced them and held out the back of my hand for them to sniff. Thankfully, they softened and then walked behind me, clipping my heels with their muzzles and growling. A groundskeeper dressed in overalls met me at the foot of the grand stairs and informed me that the mayor was finishing his Sunday paper and that I should wait on the bottom step until he was ready to meet. With a last glimpse of the sunset dropping behind the trees, I sat down heavily again, my head now pounding with the first throes of a headache.

Despite the night being hot and humid, I began to shiver: the onset of a fever. I held my head in my hands, grimaced through each minute, and waited for what felt like another hour.

When I was finally summoned to meet the mayor, I had to steady myself on the railing as an excruciating heat moved up my spine. Something was very wrong with me. Following the groundskeeper, I walked into a vast library, wall to wall with books, and was directed to sit down on an old maroon Chesterfield couch. Animal prints and African paintings adorned the walls, yet the opulence of the room was at odds with the mayor, who sat in a black leather chair, dressed in shorts and a baggy polo shirt, his stomach bulging out and his feet – adorned with a pair of dirty grey socks – up on the coffee table. An unkempt white and black beard covered his face. He looked up at me with deep contempt.

"You've ruined my Sunday evening," he said, his lip curling in disgust. He hadn't met me before, but he already hated me. Maybe it was because I was white. As we'd been learning, ever since that first border guard, Tanzania was a fiercely nationalistic country that didn't like outsiders. In social studies class I had to teach lessons about how bad the colonial nations had been in Africa.

I wondered how much Edna had been talking to him. If he had heard her side of the story, I was a young *mzungu* who had taken over in my first few weeks, decided to do everything my way, and all the staff had left because of me. Which, as I thought about it, was a pretty fair description of what had happened. But I had a chip on my shoulder about authority. It had got me in trouble often in the military, too, with many a weekend spent on extra duties as punishment.

"I'm not having such a great Sunday evening either, to be honest, so that makes two of us."

He didn't like that. He let out a grunting sigh and took off his reading glasses. His weekend newspaper was still in his hands, open to the football section on a full-page spread detailing the Friday match between Arsenal and Manchester United.

"What are you doing in that school?" he asked shortly.

I took a breath, trying to block out the worst of my headache, and then answered, "Doing my best, trying to do the best for the students, trying to – "

"That is not what I am hearing," he yelled over me. "I am hearing that you are making a total mess of things." He shook the paper in my direction, a half-page picture of Cristiano Ronaldo celebrating a goal. "So, explain yourself! What are you playing at? You think you are so clever, don't you, *mzungu*! You should not be here! You should watch your back, boy."

What followed was ten minutes of one-way traffic from the mayor, each point accentuated with an accusatory stab in my direction with his finger. He called me a coloniser. Told me that I was a white fool. That I was in big trouble. That, on his orders, the police had begun an investigation into me as being a potential USA CIA agent. That he could arrange for me to be removed with the click of his fingers. That Edna and the other teachers had come to see him a few days before, and their demands were simple. They wanted me gone and wanted things to go back to the way they were before I had come. There was no mention of Kaitlin; everyone seemed to love her still.

Maybe I should have left Buka that night. Realised that I'd got it wrong, and, with my tail between my legs, given up. Admitted defeat. As the list of people who hated me so much for coming in and changing everything continued to grow, surely I should have taken the hint. Realised that I was trying so hard to make a difference in the world that I was actually screwing things up. But I didn't think that. I didn't listen to the mayor, or Edna. I didn't allow the doubts that Kaitlin and Peters were expressing to shake my resolve.

It didn't help that as he spoke, the fever that had started a few hours earlier ripped more violently through me, and my body started to fail me. My vision began to fade first, blackness creeping in until it was tunnelled down to just in front of my eyes, and then pins and needles started to prickle through my arms and legs. My headache thumped with each word he hurled at me, and my brain felt like it was going to explode.

When he was finally out of words, he went quiet, breathing heavily. He asked me what I had to say for myself, but I didn't reply, knowing that anything I said would unleash a longer tirade from him. So, I shrugged and shook my head. Maybe surprised I wasn't fighting back, he stood up and, with a long swoop of his arm, yelled at me to leave – both his house and Buka. If I wasn't gone within two weeks, bad things would happen to me. I looked up at him, swallowed, and thanked him for his time, making my own way out. I met Frank at the front, and I struggled home with him, lacking the ability to make small chat.

When I opened the door to our home, I steeled myself and managed a thin smile at the sight of Kaitlin and Peters spending time with a group of students over cups of tea.

"What did the mayor want to talk about?" Kaitlin asked, following me into the little area we had partitioned off for our bed.

"Oh nothing. Just a chat. We talked about football mostly," I lied to her, I think for the first time. I lied because I didn't want her to worry. I lied because I didn't have the energy to speak. And I lied because I was going to get back to work the next day and pretend like I hadn't just met with the mayor. I was going to get the job done. I had to.

***

The next morning, after a feverish night, I dragged myself down the hill to Buka's pharmacy – a tin shack with a rough red cross painted on the side. After waiting on a thin wooden bench outside, I was summoned in through a faded blue shade cloth by a man wearing a grimy white coat, his name, "Andwele", written in black permanent marker above his pocket. He pricked my finger with a safety pin, smeared it roughly onto a chipped glass slide, and placed it under a lightbulb connected to a car battery. I was told to wait outside again. I closed my eyes, pink against the morning sun, small clear dots swimming against them – scratches from a childhood running through wayward branches in the bush. Ten minutes later, I was called in and told that I had malaria; +3 apparently. I asked what the maximum was, which I assumed was death.

"Plus five," Andwele responded matter-of-factly.

That's not good, I thought. I was two away from death.

But it could have been worse. I could have been +4.

Or dead.

I asked to look at my blood under the microscope and saw the ugly little asteroid-looking parasite things among the nice round blood cells fighting to keep me alive. He put three large yellow pills the size of a quarter into a small envelope made by stapling regular printer paper together.

"Take them all together. Try to eat a little bit of meat. And rest."

For years, I'd been terrified of malaria, reading about it in my Lonely Planet guides, taking antimalarial pills across New Guinea, India and the Amazon, spraying insect repellent, and wearing long sleeves and pants at night. But now that I'd had my first bout of it, I didn't feel fear. Perhaps it was because this rated as less concerning than the other things we'd already experienced. Below tribal war, curses from witch doctors and threats from the Buka mayor. Or maybe it was the tone in Andwele's voice. Or maybe because a malaria diagnosis was just another bit of crazy to add to the pile. Was I going crazy myself?

"You will be okay. Ten people have tested positive for malaria just this morning. It is the HIV/AIDS test I don't like. Those people are always fainting when they get the positive, and I only have this one bed if they fall down," he said, laughing. Then he quieted his voice and turned serious. "Mr Aaron, maybe you buy me a drink this fine morning; we go now, together."

"Ah, no, there's a line of people here that need your help. Thank you for the pills, though," I said.

"Okay, *sawa sawa*. Next time, though, right?" He winked at me.

On the way back to the school, I popped into the meat shop and ordered 100 grams of beef. The butcher hacked a small steak off the side of a fly-covered carcass hanging on a hook and wrapped it up in a page of last week's newspaper. I followed the doctor's instructions with the beef, but the bedrest was not something I could do. I took my three pills and got back to work.

- EIGHTEEN -

I SAT UP straight in bed and peered into the moonlit room, straining to hear. A rustling was coming from near the window. Probably a rat trying to get in. I didn't hear the thuds of bass from the bars, meaning it must have been a few hours after midnight. There was more rustling, and then muted voices. I reached down for my panga, a foot-and-a-half long machete with a worn-down handle, and stepped out from the false safety of our blue mosquito net. Kaitlin slept soundly next to me, still recovering from her latest bout of malaria, three for each of us now; perhaps the curses were working.

A surge of fear pulsed over me. No matter who was out there, I would make sure that nothing would happen to her. Barefoot, in only my underwear, I silently edged closer to the window and made out three shadows just outside. A hand edged in through the window – they'd cut a hole in the flyscreen – and I gritted my teeth and raised the panga high. The bars would keep them from getting through the window, but if they reached for the door locks to try to get in, they were going to lose their hand. I pulled the panga back a few inches and gritted my teeth, ready to give my first swing of the blade everything I'd got. But then there was a dull thump, then another. Someone yelled, and then people were running, both towards and away from the house.

I quickly pulled out the steel bars from across our door, opened it wide, and stood in the doorway, ready to kill anyone who wanted to try to get through to Kaitlin, who was now sitting up in bed. Dark figures ran up the path towards me. Then I lowered the knife. It was tall, proud Jelani and skinny, smart Frank. "What's going on, boys?" I whispered sharply.

"Gangsters were trying to attack you and Sister Kait, but we attacked them instead. We hit them with big rocks, and they ran away." I looked below the window where I'd heard voices and saw the two large boulders our boys had thrown. I grinned at their weapon of choice, my adrenaline giving way quickly to relief.

"Well done, guys, well done." I shook their hands as they stepped up to our door.

I heard Kaitlin's footsteps behind me and looked back to see her dressed in jeans and a t-shirt, a kanga skirt wrapped around her as a shawl. I reached around her waist and brought her in close to me, but I felt her pull away.

"Kaitlin, the boys just saved us." I saw them grow a few inches – they adored her. "I've got some sodas in here; you guys want one?" Of course, they did, even at two in the morning. They deserved to bathe in the spoils of their courage.

I wondered what was in her little retreat from me. I knew I'd lost the respect and affection of everyone else, but I wasn't losing her, was I? I shook the thought away, hoping that she was just embarrassed in front of the boys.

Jelani and Frank were two of our best students. Of the hundred on the list, there were a handful giving it their absolute all. For them the goal of passing the national exams and moving forward on the path to university was real. While we offered as much support as we could to all, for many, the new expectations and the new goals had proved too ambitious. The environment where they could spend all day hanging out, flirting, sleeping and playing games was long gone. We'd been in Buka for half a year by then, and still ran everything with just Peters, Kaitlin and me.

I put on some shorts and a t-shirt and grabbed the two sodas we had. But as the boys drank their rewards, we were interrupted by voices coming from around the corner. My panga was still close to me, but Jelani stood up and walked towards them, his confidence still high. He was back a few minutes later, his face lit up by the moonlight. But the smiles were gone; he had fear in his eyes now.

"Cecilia is very sick, Mr Aaron. We need your help," he said, and ran into the darkness.

I left the panga with Frank and followed Jelani across the compound and into the girls' dormitory. Kaitlin followed, both as an escort for us to the girls' dormitory and because it felt safer for her to be with me. We entered the first room, a rough space with a concrete floor and broken plywood walls. For months they'd been spooked by all the rumours of curses and were prone to moments of panic where they would shriek and wail and pray into the night to expel what they thought were demons in their rooms. But tonight, there were quieter, more sombre. A group was crying, and Peters was leaning down over a girl, speaking quietly in Swahili to her and waving a piece of cardboard to cool her down. It was Cecilia, one of the older girls, and she wasn't moving. I knelt beside Peters on the thin, filthy, sweat-soaked mattress and put my cheek by her mouth, unable to feel any breath. I checked for her pulse: it was barely there, a dull throb every few seconds, and I lifted one of her eyelids to see her eyeball rolled back. Her forehead was as hot as a stone in the summer sun. It was malaria – she had come down with it the week before, along with a dozen other kids. But she was clearly doing far worse than any of them.

"Did she take her malaria pills yesterday, Zuri?"

"No, Mr Aaron. She said they make her stomach painful."

I pinched my lips together, then glanced at Peters. From the look in his eyes, I knew that we were both on the same page. She only had a few hours to live. We had already been invited to two funerals in Buka, and we did not want Cecilia to be the third. She was a brilliant girl, so kind, with a dream to be a schoolteacher one day. We needed to find a clinic and get some quinine straight into her veins. I beckoned with my head to Peters and Jelani, and they reached under her armpits, and we lifted her. Her thin, stained grey singlet was drenched with sweat; her skin was as clammy as a wet blanket. I asked Kaitlin to lock herself back into our house, and she wrapped her kanga cloth around Cecilia's bare legs as I took hold of them. Lifting her up, we stumbled out of the dormitory and moved down into the slum, her body limp in our arms. With no electricity, it was dark, and other than a few figures lurking in the shadows, all was quiet. We passed shacks, dogs barking at us, baring their teeth and just daring us to come closer. Peters ran ahead to wake Andwele, the health worker who had diagnosed my first malaria round. But a few minutes later, as we neared the pharmacy, he caught back up to us, walking slowly up the path, his head low.

"Is he coming?" I whispered as we laid Cecilia down on the dusty concrete veranda at the front of the clinic. Jelani leaned over her, his long arms glistening with sweat as he waved his hand over her face in a futile but caring attempt to try to cool her down.

"No, Mr Aaron. He is not coming. He says the clinic is closed and that he will open at nine tomorrow. We must wait here until then." Peters wasn't the kind of guy who was going to push the doctor to do anything he didn't want to.

I opened my mouth to speak and then paused to try to figure out what to do. "She'll be dead by nine," I said. I jogged towards Andwele's house and banged on his door, yelling his name. I heard a murmur inside.

"*Daktari*," I said, "one of my students is very sick, and she will die in a few hours. We need your help." Then there was the sound of steel on steel as he opened the door. He reeked of the local moonshine they served in the bars. "*Hapana*." He shook his head. "*Kesho asubuhi*." He started to close the door.

"No!" I yelled, as dogs barked in the distance. My heart dropped. "Please." I grabbed his arm tightly and pulled him towards the clinic. "When tomorrow comes, she will be dead."

He looked at me hazily, then tried his luck. "*Elfu kumi*."

I shook my head, my jaw clenched. I couldn't believe he was doing this. "*Elfu tano*?"

"*Sawa sawa*," he said sleepily, moving to unlock his door.

We had just bartered for this girl's life, and I won. For five dollars.

He stumbled the hundred yards to the clinic, with me walking impatiently in front of him, and then unlocked the door. Jelani, Peters and I carried Cecilia in, laying her gently down on a thin old hospital bed. With the power out, the small light on my Nokia phone was the only light we had, and we watched as Andwele ran his hands clumsily along the sparse shelves for the supplies we needed. When he found the quinine bags, he slapped them on the thin bed next to Cecilia, along with some tubes and a needle, and sat down heavily in his chair with his eyes closed, beckoning for us to continue.

I had learned how to insert an IV in the military, but other than helping a field medic put one into my own arm when I was severely dehydrated in a rainforest of Papua New Guinea, I certainly couldn't say I was an expert.

"Andwele, come on, we need your help," I said, glaring at him. The whites of his eyes were yellow, with angry streaks of red through them. He probably had only stopped drinking a few hours ago.

"Put it straight in her head. She looks like she has cerebral malaria."

I looked at the needle and it shook in my hand. Now, that was well beyond my training.

"I think we just do the regular way, and if she needs another bag in her head, I will pay. Please talk me through it, Andwele." I was digging a hole in my lip with my teeth, willing this quinine to get into Cecilia as soon as possible. But he wasn't moving, the bastard. I had to do it.

With Peters holding the torch, and Andwele slurring his way through the instructions, I connected the bag and asked Jelani to hold it above his head. Without clean alcohol wipes, I wiped the sweat and grime off Cecilia's arm with the back of my wrist and then, holding the needle in between my fingers, I tried to calm my breathing and reduce the shake of my right hand. I clenched my teeth and sank the needle deep into her dehydrated vein, twisting the clamp to allow the liquids to flow. I watched the miracle drops of quinine solution trickle into her body. Andwele gave a drunken clap of congratulations, so I figured it must have been working. I looked at Peters, who was holding Cecilia's limp hand tight. All we could do was be patient.

After an hour, we changed the bag over, Andwele still asleep in his chair, and then waited longer still. While it dripped in, Peters and Jelani stayed with Cecilia, but I stepped outside for a break, leaning my head against a pole to stare up at the dark sky, a rare cool breeze blowing gently on my face. I felt like there was no emotion left in me – just overwhelming exhaustion from the night, the week, the year. But I couldn't sleep either, the sharp stab of cortisol zipping through my head. I thought of Kaitlin back up the hill at our house and wondered if she had remembered to lock the door shut properly. I'd left the panga with Frank, and I knew he'd be sleeping outside to protect her.

More time passed, and with it a feeling of safety with the arriving day. A man emerged out of the dull orange of the morning, pushing a wooden cart laden with potatoes. He recognised me and decided to rest the cart down in the sand, wipe the sweat off his brow, and shake my hand. It was Morris, one of the grocers in the slum. A strong, barrel-chested man dressed in clean tan trousers with a black singlet, his goatee beard and hair was always trimmed perfectly. Every few days, we visited him to buy some tomatoes to mix up the food that we had at the school.

"*Habari za asubuhi*, Mr Aaron?" he asked warmly. "Is Sister Kait sick?" We weren't religious and had never asked anyone to call her Sister Kait, but for some reason, it was how everyone in Buka referred to her. It was nice and made us feel like we had a family in the slum.

"No, Morris. One of our students. Really bad malaria," I said, my voice catching with just the tiniest break. There was an emotion I couldn't find just a moment ago. I had sat out in front of this clinic more times than I would have liked to since we had been here, either getting tested myself for malaria or sitting with Kaitlin or the students. But this felt different. I worried we might lose Cecilia. I choked it back.

"Mr Aaron, maybe she has more than malaria," he said, looking up at the halo of light towards the coast as the sun rose. No-one spoke about AIDS in the slum, but there were funerals every week. It was almost as if people thought that if they didn't utter the words, it wouldn't exist.

"No tomatoes today?" I asked, to break the silence.

"No tomatoes, they are too expensive now. I have some very fine bananas, though," he said, tapping them.

Then he changed the subject.

"Mr Aaron," he said as looked straight at me. "I try so hard to make things better for my family, but nothing seems to work. What should I do?"

I held his gaze silently for a few seconds but then leaned my head back against the post behind me, a lump building in my throat again. A year earlier, sitting in my apartment in Sydney with a glass of wine, typing up an essay for my degree in development, I would have been able to write about a policy that could help the poor. But now, here in Buka, running on empty, I didn't have an answer.

"My whole life I have worked so hard," he continued. "I tried to learn in school. I was a good student; I did my exams. I started this small shop. Now, every morning, I wake up before the sun. I push this cart through the sand, and until late, I try to sell my fruit and vegetables. I polish them so they are shining; you know it yourself. I am careful with my money. Yet I am too poor. The price of food goes up, and we can't afford anything, and now my son …" He shook his head and looked away from me, wiping the tears from his eyes with a blistered hand. "I will do anything for him to not have this life. But I don't know what to do. I try. I promise you, Mr Aaron, my whole life I try and try. Please tell me what to do."

I'd only seen my father cry once, when his brother was killed in a motorcycle accident, and no-one cried in the navy. But my chin quivered, and I began to cry, too. They came out of a desperate sympathy for Morris, out of respect for his struggles to improve his son's chances in life. But they also came out of frustration that I was out of answers. I did not know what to do for him. Since I was a kid, I'd been told that I was a quick thinker, somebody who could come up with a solution. But now, for Morris, for Cecilia, and maybe even for Buka, I was all out of hope, all out of ideas. I felt helpless in a place that needed so much help. If I really faced facts, how much of a positive impact were we really making here? When we left, it would be just as bad as it was before we arrived. All this effort was just a drop in a sea of despair.

"What do I do, Mr Aaron? What do I do for him?" he asked again. "Please, Mr Aaron. I am not asking for your money. I am asking for your advice. You are educated. Tell me what to do and I will do it," he pleaded.

I wiped at my face, but the tears came anyway.

"I don't know, Morris," I said, chewing on my cheek to try to be strong for him. "I don't know. I'm so sorry. I don't know."

We stared at each other. Two men, trying our best but losing.

But we weren't equal. Any day, I could leave Buka and return to my pick of wealthy countries to find a good job, a safe house, clean water. Morris could not.

We sat quietly on the clinic's concrete veranda as the slum's roosters began to herald in the new day – another in Buka, where some would laugh, some would cry, and all would struggle to survive.

"You are a good man, Morris," I tried, "and a great father. Your son will be a good man. And it will be because of you." I held his hands with both of mine. He let out a heavy, tired sigh.

"You are a good man, too," and he touched my shoulder lightly with his hand and wiped his tears with the other. "You have a good day, Mr Aaron. Hello to Sister Kait."

"You have a good day too, Morris. I will come by later to buy some of those fine bananas."

He picked up the handles of his cart and the old wood creaked with the weight. I watched as he walked slowly down the street, the unbalanced wheels squeaking as they fought through the soft sand. He stopped just before the corner, lowered the cart and turned around.

"What is the girl's name?" he called to me.

"Cecilia," I yelled back.

"Give these fruits to Cecilia when she wakes up," he said, throwing me two bananas. "I will pray for her."

***

The quinine performed its miracle that night on Cecilia, and we carried her back to school before midday. She rested for a few days and was in class the next week. My luck had run out with the immigration department, with my friend asking for a bribe to extend our visas once more. We were on borrowed time but figured we could do a border run to Mombasa to get us past the date when the students would be taking their national exams.

Mentally and emotionally, Kaitlin and I were running on empty, surrounded every week by hardship and death, and plagued with our own illness. Yet we were still so focused on the goal we had written on our wall – getting ten of our kids through the national exams. The darkness we were down in now felt like the test. All the times I had talked about doing something good for the world, living a life of meaning. This was it. I had to do this. If I were ever to write the wrongs of hundreds of thousands of people dying because of a military campaign I fought in, surely I could succeed in helping just ten students here in Tanzania. I didn't know who I was if I couldn't do that. What I was on this earth for. I'd almost lost myself.

And maybe I'd already lost Kaitlin too. We tried to talk but she said she was having doubts about everything we were doing. She spoke of watching my drive and determination and feeling like it wasn't her. That as things got more challenging at the school she stopped feeling like she had any solutions, but that this was made worse because I'd stopped asking for her advice. We had stopped making love, managing only an exhausted kiss before we fell asleep each night. But then that stopped as well.

I had written the Nietzsche quote, *The one who has a why to live by can bear almost any how*, on a piece of paper and stuck it above my desk. I was resilient to the point of madness. Waking up every day as things fell to pieces around me, ready to go again. I felt like if I worked harder things would improve. And that it was worth it if just one of the students made a go of it, passed the exams and had a better life.

But we'd started losing them as well. They were turning up late to school, distracted in class, and fighting with each other over small problems. Kaitlin had responded in her regular way, with love, and the students loved her in turn. My response, though, had been to push harder. It was all I knew from the military. If they were late, I didn't allow them inside. If they missed three days in a row, they had to come in with a respected member of the community to have a discussion with us. If boarders didn't help out with the tasks around the school, they didn't get dinner. I was pushing everyone, but each night, in the privacy of our little house, writing in my journal by candlelight, I found I was losing hope myself.

Late one Friday, I'd given up on my class for the week and headed back to my house. I felt like another malaria bout was coming for me, and I left my students to do whatever they wanted for the last few hours of the afternoon. I sat down at our table, my head in my hand, and then heard a barely perceptible knock on our door frame. A Peters knock. I looked up and there he was. Polite as ever. I put my mask of confidence back on and waved him in enthusiastically, offered him tea and pulled a seat over for him.

"Hapana," he shook his head. He closed the door, scanning left and right outside before he did. "Aaron, I need to be quick. You must be careful," he said earnestly. "You are my friend. Please listen to me. You need to take a break. We have all been working hard, but you are working too hard. You are sick. You are very thin. You must have some time to yourself. You must rest. Kaitlin and I will deal with the boys this week. You rest."

"No, Peters. Thank you, really, but these next few weeks are vital. Yes, I'm probably sick with malaria again, but we probably all are, right? If we get this right, a whole bunch of these kids will pass the exams." Rubbing the back of my neck with my hand, I leaned in closer to him. "Peters, this school can be amazing; we can't give up now and just take a break. If students from here get to university, it will be …"

He held up his hand to quiet me. "Aaron. You are not listening. You must take a break. You'll die."

I started to argue again, but he reached out and touched my hand, the bright whites of his eyes shining. "Aaron. I overheard some of the older boys talking about you today …" He paused for a second, playing with a loose splinter of wood on the chair, and then looked up at me again. "They say they are going to kill you tonight."

I smirked. "Kill me, Peters? Come on!"

He did not smile. "Yes. And they will do it. You know that a teacher from a school nearby was killed not so long ago. I think the boys have been listening to this story. I'm being serious, Aaron. I'm very worried. You must get away from Buka."

I took a deep breath, my headache like a small dagger underneath my right ear. My pulse slow, weary. I looked over Peters's head and tried to think of my next move. School would be out in a few minutes. I looked around our little house. My knife was under the bed, and I wondered if I should get it. There was not a whisper of wind, and the heat of the afternoon wafted lazily through the windows. The brown and purple curtains made my head spin as I looked at them. They were so damn ugly; if I got through today, I'd throw them away. The bright Barclays Bank Blue paint that we had put on the walls around the school suddenly made me feel sick. A student walked past outside, and anger swelled in me – I wondered if he was one of the kids who was readying to kill me. I saw the pathetic little bougainvillea I had planted outside, fighting desperately to survive in the rocky, white dust of Buka, a few shoots of green trying to emerge from dry twigs. Then I stood, caught my balance. As I walked to the door, I saw Kaitlin stepping out of a class with a handful of notebooks, coming my way.

Students were streaming out of their classrooms now. The end of the day.

She couldn't know what Peters had just told me. My mind shifted woozily from delirium to focus. *Figure this out, Aaron.*

"Okay. Don't tell Kaitlin what you've just told me. In fact, can you please look after her this afternoon?"

I walked out of the house, towards her, still as beautiful through a year of malnutrition and malaria as the day I met her on that beach in Spain. I kissed her on the lips, for the first time in a while, and hugged her. Horrifically, for a split second I wondered if it was the last time I ever would hold her, and my mind screamed at me to just run away with her and never return.

"Peters just stopped by; he wants to catch up with you. He's got some tea on. I'll be back in a bit." She asked me if I was okay – we were never affectionate like this in front of the students, but unable to speak, I nodded. Ahead of me, Jelani came out of class.

"Jelani, I need all the boys to meet me in this room in ten minutes," I said, more sternly than I'd ever spoken to him.

"*Sawa sawa.*" He was cold with me, and I wondered if he knew something. I stepped into the empty classroom and tried to bring my thoughts together. I was breathing too quickly, tapping each finger with my thumb. I'd come a damn long way to try to help here in Buka. To challenge the theories I had learned about in university with the truest realities of poverty. We'd been threatened by the mayor. The police were investigating us. The immigration department wanted us out of their country. We had been riddled with malaria for what felt like an age, enduring fevers, pain that would tear down our spines and headaches that felt like a chainsaw moving through our skulls. Most of our staff had left, and some hated us so much that they'd paid witch doctors to put curses on us – ten was the latest rumour. Through it all, I reassured Kaitlin and myself that it was worth it if the kids still cared. If their futures would be brighter because of our hard work.

But now they wanted me dead.

Part of me thought that it wasn't worth it anymore. I was exhausted and out of ideas. I'd failed. I sat at a desk at the front of the classroom as boys started moving in. Was everything we'd done here a waste of time? Nothing more than an interesting interlude for a school that would return to anarchy soon after we left. I felt sweat pouring out of me, a cocktail of humidity and corrosive adrenaline as the older ones, the young men, filed in and sat on seats and desks. Within a few minutes, there were thirty or so. Jelani stood tall near the back, not making eye contact with me.

"Jelani, can you please lock that door?" I asked. He pursed his lips and nodded his head coolly. The whole room turned to watch him pull across the latch.

I stood up. "Okay, men," I started, my voice loud, coming from the top of my chest. I scanned the room, looking at all of the faces in front of me. Young men that I had laughed with. Frank, who had come so far in such a short time. Jelani, a born leader. And then other boys, hardened young men who were already primed for a life on the streets and hustling their way to survive. I had worked late into the night with so many of them. Now none of them wanted to look at me.

"The rumour is that some of you want to kill me tonight." My breath moved to my nose; I felt my pulse quicken in my neck. Many of them were looking down, but others were staring straight at me, anger in their eyes. I was angry, too. Furious. My head felt hot, my palms sweating, and I tasted metal in my mouth. It was blood, I'd bitten my lip so hard. I'd gone off the edge.

"Well, I don't want Kaitlin to see that happen …"

I looked around the room, and my eyes rested on where I guessed the threat was coming from, a group of students who were glaring back at me, rage shooting from their eyes.

"So kill me now."

Some of the younger boys looked around, confused, while the tougher group turned away from me, muttering something to themselves. But then silence. No movement. My lips were pursed tightly together. I'd never felt so despised.

"Let's do it!" I yelled. "Kill me!"

If they wanted to run at me with the knives that I knew some of them carried in their pockets, they would overpower me. But no-one moved. We were all frozen. Still but for the rise and fall of our chests.

Then all the tension in me snapped. That tightness I'd felt, right back from that night on the diving course. When I'd watched those planes fly into the Twin Towers on television. The hate I'd taken with me to Iraq and the guilt and trauma I'd come home with. I felt my last ounce of strength drain from me, like an exhausted fighter giving up in the last round. My fists, too heavy to keep up, then unclenched.

And my soul whispered quietly to me. *Don't be strong, Aaron. Take heart. Listen. Listen to them!* I sat down heavily on a chair, the wooden legs loose. My breathing was shallow and strained, and I felt my shoulders rising and falling.

"I'm sorry," I said quietly. "I'm sorry," I repeated. "I'm sorry." I leaned forward, gripping the front of my chair. "For everything. I'm so sorry." I was talking to them. But also to Farooq. To the nameless many in Iraq who had suffered and died because of people like me, men who had become so fixated on fighting the monsters that they became monsters themselves.

We all sat there in silence. I hoped Jelani would speak; he always had something to say. The tin roof creaked and cracked with the hot afternoon breeze.

Timothy spoke first. "Yes, we are angry," he said, pushing his way to the front of his friends, his voice raised. "We feel like this idea of yours, of this becoming a great school, of all of us getting through exams, going to university… we feel like it is your idea. We don't think it's possible. And you push, push, push us!" he said, slapping one hand on the other before continuing. "But maybe we are not clever? Maybe we can't do it? Maybe we will always be poor? People like you come and promise everything, and then you leave. And you will go back to your rich country. Before you came, no-one cared if we hung around. No-one cared if we were late. No-one cared about anything. Just leave us alone." He sat down heavily, high-fiving some of his friends as he did.

He was right. Maybe all of this was more for me than them. My sick crusade. A selfish shot for retribution and peace.

But that was just the start of it.

For the next hour, I sat in silence and listened to them as they spoke. Most of them, even the youngest ones, said that they didn't think they would ever pass their exams. They talked about returning to the streets, joining gangs, getting jobs as conductors on the public minivans. Life had been so tough for them. Pain, frustration and neglect were a part of their daily existence. It felt to me that their spending a few years at this school was just an escape before they needed to face up to the tough realities of poverty that they'd resigned themselves to. It was clear to the boys that the odds were in my favour as a white, privileged man, and stacked against them. It was the same desperation I'd heard from Morris the night Cecilia had been sick. Trying to impose my values and my solutions on the people of Buka was so flawed. I didn't know how to solve the problems of Buka. Of course I didn't. I came from a different world. It didn't matter how hard I worked; change was not going to come from me in Buka. Change had to come from these kids. From the teachers at this school. From the people who wanted change here more than I – an outsider – could ever want that change. Person by person, family by family, community by community. Maybe that was how the world changed. With local people standing up in the toughest places and deciding to make change right where they were. With what they had. Maybe it was time for outsiders like me to shut up in places like this, and step back for once. To let some local leaders step up.

After they were all talked out, it went silent again. I waited a little longer and then spoke slowly.

"Okay. So what do you want to do? I can leave today if you want. I'll pack up right now and Kaitlin and I will go. Or if you want us to stay, we'll give you everything we've got for these last few months of the year before the government kicks us out. It's your school now."

- NINETEEN -

We were leaving in the morning, and I knew I should have been packing, but I was on a roll. I looked up from my notepad, which was covered in notes – the early strategy for an organisation we'd been dreaming up each night. We were going to call it Spark*, and its mission was simple: "Backing local change." We would raise money to support local social entrepreneurs in some of the poorest places in the world across Africa, Asia and the Pacific. For too long, foreigners like us had come in holding the money, and with their own ideas on how to change things. But we were going to flip that and provide as much support as we could to local changemakers, people just starting out but with a great idea. People who weren't used to getting support. They were these sparks of brilliance, and we were the fuel that could help them grow. We didn't know how we were going to raise the money; neither of us had skills in fundraising or had rich friends or family, but we'd figure that out. We had a big goal already. A million people living in poverty would have their lives changed. People would have jobs, kids would go to school, sick people would get access to care, homes would be built and improved. And the heroes of the story would be these local entrepreneurs.

"How are you doing?" I asked Kaitlin,

"I've felt better." She forced out a smile. Her resilience had blown me away so many times since we'd been in Africa, but now she was dangerously thin and the latest bout of malaria that she'd been battling for weeks was making her weaker than I'd ever seen her. I barely weighed 120 pounds. She was well under 100. A year in Buka had almost defeated us. She rolled up her one pair of pants and tucked them into her bag.

But the school felt different from when we arrived. The buildings had been repaired, the farm was producing crops, a great local teaching team came in every day, supporting hundreds of students. Some of those students, fourteen of them, had passed their senior exams and were moving into their final two years of school at a nearby college before university. Margaret would continue supporting them. They were heroes to the other students, and we hoped that the success they'd worked so hard for was contagious for the students coming behind them. We were thrilled by what had been achieved but also exhausted.

That day with the boys, when they'd threatened to kill me and I had confronted them, had been the turning point. They'd taken control and I'd invited Peters and Kaitlin in to watch as they, and the girls, wrote a new vision for the school and their lives. For how they would study, how they would treat each other, and how they would work together to sit the exams when they were ready. They told me, Peters and Kaitlin what our jobs would be, to teach every day and to do so as part of the team. One by one, they'd come up and signed the statement on the board in chalk. We all walked out together, and they made the decision to slaughter one of the chickens to cook a pilau rice. Their call, they were in charge.

After surviving five bouts of malaria, death threats, curses from witch doctors and furious threats from Edna and Mayor that never seemed to amount to much, it was the immigration department that had finally finished us off. We managed our one final extension of our visas with a midnight border run to Mombasa before the game was up and we were given the dreaded stamp that told us we had to leave the country.

But it wasn't all bad news. We were returning to the rolling hills of Makuyu, which felt like the land of milk and honey. No malaria, clean drinking water, and trees heavy with avocados and mangoes. It was time to see Asha at the microfinance bank we'd started together. She had done an amazing job supporting Mary and all of her devoted savers to hit their goals. I was returning with their interest top-ups, and a pile of new kanga skirts I'd picked up in Nairobi. The push–pull experiment had also been a huge success, improving crop yields by 300 per cent, and it was ready to expand.

We were travelling by bus tomorrow, and wanting to move lightly, we had given away much of what we owned over the last few days. Rumours of our generosity had spread among the students, and many of them had come knocking on our door, politely asking us if we had anything else to give away. For some reason, our t-shirts had been the hottest item, as old, dirty and torn as they were. We'd initially given some of them away without thinking, but their status in the fashion stakes of the school had soared, and the students had been bartering to try to secure one. Those lucky few owners hadn't taken them off in days.

"Should I keep this?" I grinned as I held up the grey, second-hand XXXL polo shirt that had been an unclaimed item of clothing earlier in the year. Its journey to Africa had probably started with great intentions in a donation bin in a place like Florida, but when none of the kids or community members had wanted it or been big enough to fill it out, it had ended up on the top of the burn pile before I rescued it. Some terrible clothes had made their way to the project, but this one was a personal favourite of mine. Whenever we had malaria, it made Kaitlin and me laugh to put it on, as long as a muumuu dress, and it had been given its own special name – the sick shirt.

"No!" she laughed. She grabbed it and threw it to the other side of our little house. "God, I hope I never see that ridiculous sick shirt again! Besides, I promised Peters that he could have it. He wants to keep it as a reminder of us."

We were interrupted by a knock on the door. It was late, and the thick security bars I had installed were already slid across.

"It's Zuri," we heard from outside. "Sister Kait said I should come around tonight before bed."

I opened the door to see her delightful face smiling back at me.

"Zuri!" Kaitlin exclaimed, tapping the seat next to her. She stepped in, dragging her polio damaged foot across the floor and sitting down. She brought her strong hand together with her twisted weaker one and rested them both in her lap. "Great! I asked you around tonight because I wanted to give you something."

Zuri's eyes were full of excitement.

"You have been such a special friend to me while I have been here, and I hope we never forget each other," Kaitlin continued. Now Zuri was beaming, adjusting her kanga and desperately trying to keep her erupting smile under control, pushing her top lip down over her teeth. I watched as Kaitlin reached into the pocket of her jeans and pulled out a small necklace with a charm on it. Zuri's face dropped.

"A close friend gave me this necklace many years ago," she said, holding it up and letting the pendant hang down. "It says here in Swahili – *Rafiki*. 'Friend.' It's for you, my friend." Kaitlin handed it to Zuri with a smile, and she took the necklace in her hand, and looked down at it, her face a mix of confusion and disappointment. She peered up at Kaitlin, then down at the necklace again, this time for a few seconds more.

I heard her nervously begin, "Sister Kait, thank you for this necklace, I like it very much. You are my best friend, and I will miss you so much." She was still looking down. "But see, Sister Kait, me myself, I really wanted a t-shirt."

A slightly frustrated smile passed across Kaitlin's face. "But Zuri, doesn't our friendship mean more to you than a t-shirt?" she said, her voice a little weak. "A t-shirt will wear out, and you will grow out of it. But this you can keep forever. We can remember each other." She sounded tired, like she was running on fumes. Zuri didn't respond, still looking down at the necklace.

I stood up and moved towards the door. "Okay, Zuri, thank you so much for coming. We will see you in the morning before we catch the bus. *Usiku mweme.*"

She stood up. "Good night to you, too, Mr Aaron and Sister Kait."

I closed the door quietly behind Zuri and turned to look at Kaitlin. She was still smiling, but there was a sadness there.

"Are we really nothing more than a t-shirt to these kids?" she said as she looked down at her bag. "After everything ... please tell me that this year has meant something more than that."

"Kaitlin, of course it has. Think about everything – " I began, but a knock at the door interrupted me. I hadn't locked it yet. Surely it wasn't someone coming for another t-shirt.

"Mr Aaron, it's Frank. Can I speak with you?"

Frank had proved to be an amazing friend and student. He'd protected us when the robbers had tried to break in and stood guard for Kaitlin that night Cecilia had been sick. He'd walked me home from the mayor's house when I'd first fallen ill with malaria. He'd come to the school from a very poor farming community in the dry centre of the country at the start of the year, knowing barely any English. There was something unique about him. Kaitlin and I had often said he had shining eyes – a little glint of promise that made us think he would really do something with his life. I had appointed him the director of farming, and one day, as we were sweating side by side, ploughing the fields, he had leaned on his djembe, his young hands already callused, and told me that his dream was to graduate from university in agricultural science so he could go back to his community to help. The saying that it takes a village to raise a child was a nice one, but we had hopes that a child like him could go back one day and raise up his village. He was the goalkeeper for the school football team, and he would pick up his study notes when the play was down the other end, meaning we'd all have to yell at him when the ball was coming his way.

Frank had passed his exams.

He was on track for university and to be the agricultural scientist he dreamed of being.

I loved him like a younger brother, but tonight we were exhausted, and not ready for another request for a t-shirt.

I opened the door and spoke before he could. "Hi, Frank. If you are after a t-shirt, *pole sana*, but we are all out, buddy."

"Hi, Frank," Kaitlin said, smiling as ever, a softer touch.

"*Mambo*, Sister Kait, *mambo*, Mr Aaron," he replied, using the less formal street slang, always trying to be cool despite his bookish tendencies.

"Yeah, so sorry, Frank, no more t-shirts. We just gave away – " Kaitlin started.

Frank held up his hand, cutting her short. Always the gentleman, he had never interrupted her before.

"I didn't come for a t-shirt," he said, swallowing hard. He paused for a second, his eyes welling up. "I came to say thank you. To both of you. Thank you for changing my life." He turned around and began to walk into the darkness. But then he stopped and turned around to look at me.

"And Aaron, one more thing." He wasn't calling me "Mr Aaron" anymore.

"You are forgiven."

I hesitated. "What do you mean?"

"You know what I mean. You are forgiven now."

He turned around and walked into the darkness. We would never see him again and we don't know what came of him.

I closed the door, putting up the bars into their holdings one by one. I reached for Kaitlin, and we sobbed. I hugged her, both of us holding on tight.

"Yes," I sighed. "This year meant something."

- TWENTY -

MIDNIGHT. DANGEROUSLY WELL past.

Downtown Nairobi.

My knees bounced with anticipation.

My hands were doing that thing they do when I was readying myself – my thumb touched each finger (little, ring, middle, index), a scar on each knuckle a little chapter of my story so far.

We were in a *matatu*, the public minivans of Kenya that were always overcrowded, usually with that heady stench of spices, body odour and diesel. The side door opened with a loud screech of tired steel. We'd just returned from a month in Europe, paid for by a surprise $6,000 the navy had sent me. It was some sort of transition payment that they'd missed. We'd found $250 return flights to London, so cheap because tourists were still too scared to come after the violence. I'd spent $1,000 on an engagement ring for Kaitlin, and in the Rodin gardens of Paris, my heart racing with emotion, I got down on one knee and proposed. She said yes, and we celebrated with the cheapest bottle of Bordeaux on the list and a shared bowl of boeuf bourguignon, followed by chocolate mousse at Le Coup Chou in the Latin Quarter. In London, we collected our mail and I opened an envelope that told me I had been offered a position in a master's program at Cambridge University. Ten months from now I would start my studies, writing a thesis focused on how to scale locally innovative solutions to poverty. The goal was that the Cambridge degree would give our Spark* charity idea a higher level of credibility for fundraising. Which we'd already started, chipping in $1,000 of that navy money, the rest saved to get us through the year.

Both a few kilos heavier and giddy in newly engaged bliss, we had returned to Nairobi. We would be spending the year back in Makuyu until it was time to move to England.

Earlier that day we had headed to the town hall to get married, which had been a farce. We lined up with another fifty couples, all sweating in our best clothes. When our turn came, late in the afternoon, an usher yelled "Tait!" into the crowd, and we walked proudly into the ceremony room, placing the rings on the table. Kaitlin used her engagement ring, and she'd found me a plastic ring at the markets.

"Don't put it on the table; put it on her finger," the celebrant said, not looking at us when it was finally our turn, "and say, 'I, Aaron, marry Kaitlin'."

Letting out a breath and trying to take a moment to respect the gravity of it all, I said the words and slid Kaitlin's ring onto her finger.

"Do the same to him," the celebrant sighed, still working through her papers.

"You're married; sign here," she said, pointing to a spot on the certificate in front of her. I seized the moment and kissed Kaitlin, a bold dip to honour the romance of it all.

"Sign here!" the celebrant interrupted, and I obeyed, but then told Kaitlin to wait and not sign the certificate – the name for the bride had been incorrectly written, the name of our witness, "Edith Njeri Muigai", taking that important position. When we challenged it, the celebrant was short with us and told us to sign anyway. "The front office will figure it out," she said, which they gladly did with an eraser and some clicks on the typewriter. So, I'd walked into the wedding room unmarried, walked out married to the wrong woman, and then walked out of the building married to Kaitlin, albeit with a fraudulent-looking certificate. We found the nearest bar and celebrated with some goat meat, kachumbari salad and Tusker lagers, unable to stop looking at each other and the rings on our fingers.

But time had gotten away from us. And now we were heading for our regular guesthouse in a *matatu*, hoping we would get there safely. Kaitlin spun her new engagement ring around, hiding the small diamond ring. Clever.

As we pulled into the central bus area, our van wove through the others. It was as wild and dangerous a party as it always was, a loud, brash competition to see who had the coolest *matatu* van. And nirvana for criminals.

I stepped out just after the conductor. My backpack was on my left shoulder, and I reached for Kaitlin's. As I did, I felt a hand stab into the pocket of my jeans, where I had a few thousand shillings, about twenty bucks. But he'd picked poorly. This was the side where I used to wear my pistol, and a thousand times I'd practised how to mess someone up if they grabbed it. Habit kicked in, and I pinned the hand into my pocket, a shot of anger pulsing through me… But then I released it. The pickpocket spun around and ran away. There was still a bit of a fighter in me, but it was fading. I was more accepting of what this thief's life was like, and why he was trying to rob someone like me. The conductor held out his fist for a bump and laughed at me, saying in local Sheng slang, "*Poa-poa msee.*" He liked what he had seen.

I reached in again for Kaitlin's bag, and we set off at a quick walk. She lifted a scarf to cover her blonde hair and I pulled on the black cap I'd tucked into my belt. She brought the fingers of her right hand in between mine and moved quickly. We were good at keeping a low profile in Africa now. The nervous fear we had held a year earlier had subsided slightly, mostly replaced by a harder-edged knowledge of how to stay alive in this life we had chosen as ours. Our usual place for a bed was five minutes away at a quick pace, but it was through one of the more notorious parts of the city. On streets like these, we had seen police shooting into protestors with shotguns. We'd seen men murder the unlucky driver of a *matatu* right next to us and a mob tear a thief into pieces. We passed groups of drunken men spilling out of bars. Night girls, most of them likely HIV-positive, stumbled in high heels, looking for their next shillings. Blank-faced street kids squatted in their rags, sniffing glue from cloudy glass jars.

As we neared the guesthouse, out of the corner of my eye, I saw a man lying motionless in the gutter, a pool of blood glistening in the streetlight. A group of shadows were walking away from him. From habit, I wanted to stop and help, put my old trauma medical training to good use, but the night watchman recognised us and waved at us to hurry, unlocking the clunky old padlocks of the front door to allow us in, his thick wooden club in his hand.

"*Karibu sana*," he said nervously, his eyes bloodshot with fatigue.

"*Asante*," Kaitlin and I said, nodding, both shaking his hand.

At the top of a set of dimly lit stairs, we were greeted by a smiling face we also knew well. She had new braids in her hair since the last time we had stayed. We slid 1,000 shillings under the bars, and she passed back a key to our regular room, which, if things were as usual, would have bloodstains on the sheets, giant mosquitoes on the walls and, if we were fortunate, a few minutes of hot water from the shower. We walked down the hallway, turned the key to our door and stepped into our tiny room, the fluorescent light flickering playfully on and off, first dancing to the beats of the nightclub below and then giving up entirely.

I closed the door behind us. We placed our bags on the ground, and I looked at Kaitlin, beautiful in the passing headlights that danced through our windows. This woman who I had met on the beaches of Spain and had fallen more in love with on a Fijian island, in the nightclubs of Sydney, the hallways of the United Nations in New York and, this last year, in a Tanzanian township.

We would head back to Makuyu village tomorrow to get back to work. There was a community bank to grow. A new farm to plant. Two new buildings would go up, home to another fifty orphans. This was where we wanted to live life. At the extremes. No longer just trying to do some good, but actually doing it, equipped with a new way. A better way.

We both took in a breath of air. We were safe.

I'll never forget that moment for the rest of my life. Her face as the lights of Nairobi flickered across it. Beauty and courage in her eyes. A soundtrack of sirens and gunshots.

Maybe it was the wild thrill that came with willingly returning to one of the most dangerous cities in the world. Or that we had realised, at the same moment, that for the first time in our lives we were exactly where we wanted to be, doing exactly what we wanted to do. Whatever it was, it felt good. Without speaking, our clothes came off and we made love with a new urgency and intensity.

There would be new horizons to explore.

But right there, we were at peace.

In love. With each other, and with life, so large, so loving, full of force, grace and wonder, and good.

We held the other close.

Our two hearts, one.

– ACKNOWLEDGEMENTS –

Firstly, thank you for reading this book and coming along for the adventure. If you enjoyed the journey, the greatest gift you can give to this author is to share it with someone who you think might like it too. Another beautiful gift, rarely asked for but oh so very helpful, is if you can write a review somewhere online. I promise that I'll read it. I promise that it makes a difference.

While my name is on the cover, there are so many people who helped to bring this book to life and who I must thank.

First of all, thank you, Alexis Washam at Verto Literary. You are such a talented editor, and your structural contributions pushed, challenged and inspired me. This would be a shadow of the book it has become had you not agreed to be involved. Michael McConnell, your graceful and precise copy edits helped to bring clarity to the tale. Nina Karnikowski, thank you for stepping in at just the right time to help move this project from a decade of tinkering to becoming something real. Peter Windrim, you were an early reader who took the time, lying on your couch with a pencil behind your ear, to dive right into the adventures of "Spud" and your insights and ideas were so appreciated. Thank you, Zoe Gameau, for your actor's eye as you read chapters on the porch in Byron Bay, and Marcus Jacometti for your artist's encouragement over the years as we sat in the plantation chairs and I poured out my fears and hopes as an author. Patrick Lindsay, thank you for the coffee and phone calls, which gave small course corrections along the way. I'm grateful to Andy Kuper, my mentor for a decade, and the person who told me on the Bronte cliffs, "You won't be able to think about much else until you write this story."

To my publishing team at Hardie Grant, thanks for taking a bet on an author in an era when fewer and fewer men are reading (something I hope we can be part of turning around). Courtney Nicholls, you were always so warm and open with me, and Shahirah Hambali, you have a lovely talent for helping an author move through this often nerve-racking process of getting our books onto shelves. Amy Daoud, you created such a beautiful cover, thank you.

Over the years, a few people have given me the time and encouragement to write. Thank you to Dave Faulkner. Not only did we build a great organisation together, but so often you gave me the space and encouragement to create. In more recent years, Sean Carroll, Colin Pidd and the ByMany team, thank you for allowing me moments as an author while I joined your vision of leadership for a better world.

Mum, without those trips through the rain to the library in Browns Bay, I don't think my wonder for literature would be as strong as it is today. Thank you. Dad, I still remember you sitting on the floor of my bedroom as you interpreted a John Donne poem for me with a tear in your eye, so thank you for instilling the writer's spirit in me. Your book is next in the family, and I'll be the first one to buy a copy. To both of you, I've sometimes wondered if any of what you read in here will be tough to take, but I truly hope not. I've been as raw, honest and real as I can, and through it all, I love you both very much.

Atlas and Finn, my own boys, I hope that one day you will pick up this book, read it, and learn a little more about your father and his efforts to live with a far horizon. I love you both so very much.

Kaitlin. Love of my life, and the creator of life with me, the greatest thank you is for you. Kotahitanga.

– ABOUT THE AUTHOR –

From war zones to slums, Aaron Tait has worked across the globe as a military officer, humanitarian and social entrepreneur, and now writes to help people live deliberate lives filled with purpose. Aaron was thrust into the frontline of international crisis at a young age, deploying to Iraq immediately after 9/11 as a military officer. His travels across the world in his twenties led to a move to East Africa at twenty-five, where he led aid projects in crisis zones and urban slums. As a co-founder of the impact organisation *ygap*, Aaron has helped to improve the lives of more than a million people living in poverty. He is a geography graduate of the University of Cambridge and holds three master's degrees in international affairs. Aaron lives with his wife, Kaitlin, and his two sons, Atlas and Finn, in Byron Bay.